CHARITIES AND NOT-FOR-PROFIT ADMINISTRATION AND GOVERNANCE HANDBOOK

Donald J. Bourgeois

In Association with

Canadian Centre for Philanthropy ™
Le Centre canadien de philanthropie ᴹᶜ

Butterworths ™
A Member of the LexisNexis Group

Charities and not-for-profit administration and governance handbook

November 2001

The *Butterworth Group of Companies*

Canada:
75 Clegg Road, MARKHAM, Ontario L6G 1A1
and
1721-808 Nelson St., Box 12148, VANCOUVER, B.C. V6Z 2H2
Australia:
Butterworths Pty Ltd., SYDNEY
Ireland:
Butterworth (Ireland) Ltd., DUBLIN
Malaysia:
Malayan Law Journal Sdn Bhd, KUALA LUMPUR
New Zealand:
Butterworths of New Zealand Ltd., WELLINGTON
Singapore:
Butterworths Asia, SINGAPORE
South Africa:
Butterworth Publishers (Pty.) Ltd., DURBAN
United Kingdom:
Butterworth & Co. (Publishers) Ltd., LONDON
United States:
LEXIS Publishing, CHARLOTTESVILLE, Virginia

National Library of Canada Cataloguing in Publication Data

Bourgeois, Donald J.
Charities and not-for-profit administration and governance handbook

Includes index.
ISBN 0-433-43076-1

1. Directors of corporations — Legal status, laws, etc. — Canada. 2. Nonprofit organizations — Law and legislation — Canada. I. Title.

KE1373.B667 2001 346.71'064 C2001-903154-8

Printed and bound in Canada

PREFACE

Governance has become a big issue for charitable and not-for-profit organizations in recent years. The fact is that it always has been important but greater emphasis has been placed on "good governance" in the 1990s as we enter the twenty-first century.

There are probably a number of reasons for the emphasis. Certainly one has been the perception that there are problems with the governance of organizations. For some, the identification of problems has been an ideological matter; for others, based on experiences. Undeniably, there have been problems in the sector, the extent of which is not always readily known or determinable. A related second reason may be that governance issues have been important in other areas of society — including the for-profit sector and business corporations, government and the agencies of government — which have also experienced similar problems. As the public demands better governance in other areas of Canada, it does so with the charitable and not-for-profit sector.

Another reason may simply be the maturing and increased sophistication of organizations. Greater demands have been placed on charitable and not-for-profit organizations in the last 20 years by society as governments and businesses restructure. Historically, these organizations have always been involved — and at times played very substantial roles in the provision of health care, education (primary, secondary and university), arts and cultural life, international aid and so forth.

Nevertheless, since the late 1980s, there has been a concerted movement towards increased involvement of charitable and not-for-profit organizations in the economic and social life of Canada. The structure of the involvement has changed and is continuing to change. These changes mean that it is necessary to look at how organizations are governed and whether or not they operate in an effective and efficient manner.

This text attempts to assist directors, officers and senior management of charitable and not-for-profit organizations to address the "governance" issue. The first chapter discusses the role of directors in managing the organization. Directors are legally responsible for the management of the affairs of the organization and have various fiduciary and other duties to do so. Chapter 2 reviews a number of tools of governance, including planning and financial tools.

Risk is inherent in life and chapter 3 examines the importance of managing risk, identifies areas of risk and provides some methods to minimize risk. Chapter 4 reviews the management of the organization's assets to avoid risks to the assets. Without those assets, the organization would not be able to fulfill its objectives. Management of the organizational structure is discussed in Chapter 5. All organizations should periodically review their structure to ensure that it works for it and allows the organization to meet its objectives.

The appendix includes several policy statements and guidelines that may be useful to organizations. As with any precedent, they are intended to be examples and not to be the answer for all organizations. An organization that does not have an executive director likely will not need to have a formal performance appraisal policy; but the issues identified in that document may nonetheless be helpful to an organization to ensure that management and operational requirements are addressed.

This text is the second in a series being published by Butterworths Canada. The Canadian Centre for Philanthropy has supported the series since its inception. I would like to thank in particular Gordon Floyd and Peter Broder for their support and comments. Terry Carter, Carter & Associates, has also been very helpful, especially permitting me to draw on his own work in this area.

Finally, I would like to thank my spouse, Susan Campbell, for her ongoing support. And, of course, Daphne who now has her own house, but still prefers to sleep on the bed.

TABLE OF CONTENTS

Chapter 1

DIRECTORS AND THEIR ROLE IN MANAGING THE ORGANIZATION

A. INTRODUCTION

The directors are any organization's primary asset. This statement may seem to be inconsistent with other pronouncements on what is most important. For example, it is common for private sector, public sector and voluntary sector employers to state that their employees or volunteers are their greatest assets. Others argue that an organization's major asset is its reputation.[1] All of these statements and others are likely accurate in general and for specific organizations.

Directors are, however, unique. An organization is a legal artifice. It exists in law and as a legal concept for practical purposes. An organization allows people to structure their internal relationships and external dealings with others in an efficient and effective manner. Nobody can touch, feel, see or hear an organization; it has no physical reality. It becomes real through the actions of people. And directors are responsible for making sure that the organization relates to people in accordance with the law, that it acts in a fiscally prudent manner and that it is effective in achieving its purposes.

The organization itself may exist as a separate legal entity. Corporations, for example, are established by law as "legal persons". A large number of organizations, however, have no or little "legal personalty". These organizations are unincorporated associations which are not legally "persons". In some cases, the common law or statutory law

---

1 The importance of "reputation" and acting such that the reputation of the organization is maintained and enhanced is discussed in D.J. Bourgeois, *Charities and Not-for-Profit Fundraising Handbook* (Toronto: Butterworths Canada Ltd., 2000) at 2-6.

does recognize a limited legal personalty to these unincorporated associations, for specific purposes. In other cases, the organizations may be "trusts", in which the assets are held in trust by legal persons, such as individuals or corporations.

Regardless of the legal structure, it takes real people for an organization to act. The law — in the form of the courts, regulators and governments — and the public look to directors and officers as the primary method by which organizations act and for accountability purposes. The law and the public have developed expectations that directors and officers will ensure that the organization achieves its goals, complies with the law that applies to the organization and operates in a fiscally prudent and effective, efficient manner. The method for doing so is often called "governance".

A number of governments in Canada have taken steps to improve governance in organizations. The Government of Canada is doing so in partnership with the voluntary sector over several years.[2] Provincial levels of government, such as British Columbia and Ontario have also been involved in policy and program development in this area, with varying degrees of commitment.[3]

The issue is of importance because without a strong voluntary sector with organizations that have in place appropriate governance and accountability structures much of what makes Canada a strong and "civil" society would not be possible. Governments recognize this fact and have slowly begun to take action to support the sector. For example, British Columbia's Ministry of Community Development, Cooperatives and Volunteers provides programs and services to support the voluntary sector as part of the government's overall policy objectives.

---

[2] See *Engaging the Voluntary Sector*, Voluntary Sector Task Force, Privy Council Office of the Government of Canada, February 18, 1999; and *Partnering for the Benefit of Canadians: Government of Canada – Voluntary Sector Initiative*, Voluntary Sector Task Force, Privy Council Office, June 9, 2000.

[3] For example, *The Ontario Voluntary Forum – Growing Our Future*, September 1998. British Columbia issued a Draft Strategy, *Promoting the Volunteer and Community Services Sector in British Columbia*, January 28, 1999. These activities followed the Ontario Law Reform Commission's *Report on the Law of Charities* (Toronto: Queen's Printer, 1996); and *Helping Canadians Help Canadians: Improving Governance and Accountability in the Voluntary Sector*, a discussion paper issued by the Panel on Accountability and Governance in the Voluntary Sector, May 1998. Several foundations have also been involved in promoting informed discussion of governance issues, carrying out research and in developing approaches for governance. The Muttart Foundation, J.W. McConnell Family Foundation, Vancouver Foundation and Kahanoff Foundation have been particularly supportive in this area.

B APPROACHES TO GOVERNANCE

The legal, governmental and public expectations of organizations are articulated and summarized in a number of ways — but they always focus on the organization and how it is governed by its directors. The terms "governance" and "stewardship" are used in *Building on Strength: Improving Governance and Accountability in Canada's Voluntary Sector.*[4] This seminal report was the work of a panel of distinguished Canadians with experience and knowledge of the voluntary sector. The panel was established by several national organizations to provide guidance on governance and accountability. The report is seminal because it became the basis for ongoing work in modernizing the voluntary sector and its regulatory framework, and for making it more effective.

"Governance" for the panel is a combination of both the overall processes and the structures that are used in directing and managing the organization's operations and activities. "Stewardship" is the responsibility of the board of directors of an organization and involves the active oversight by the board of the organization's governance. These two concepts are easily stated, but a great deal is packed into them — something that is readily apparent by the length and complexity of the panel's report and background materials.

The need for such a panel grew out of several dynamics that were at play in Canada (and throughout the world) in the late 20th century. Most of these dynamics were and remain beyond the control of the voluntary sector as a whole and certainly of individual organizations. The panel was struck in part to help the sector to respond to these dynamics and to provide guidance to organizations on how to do so. These dynamics include:

- changing role of government from a service deliverer and direct provider of services to a standard setter;
- the downloading of what had been government activities and functions onto the voluntary sector and the private sector. The federal, provincial, territorial and municipal levels of government may each take their own approach, but "alternative service delivery" and "private/public partnerships" are clearly the trend;
- changing social and economic realities facing communities and groups within communities — not the least of which are the impact

4 Panel on Accountability and Governance in the Voluntary Sector, Final Report, (Ottawa: February 1999).

of the "new economy", "globalization" and new international structures;

- an increasingly diverse population and cultural backgrounds in Canada;
- a movement from philanthropy by the private sector towards "sponsorships" and marketing;
- a reduction in overall support by governments of organizations and a refocusing of what remains from core-funding to project funding. This dynamic together with the movement away from philanthropy by the private sector appears to have led many organizations towards activities that will receive funding but which may or may not be consistent with the organization's and its members sense of priorities;
- increased competition in the "charity" marketplace — be it for grants from governments or foundations, contracts for the delivery of services, donations and sponsorships from businesses, donations by individuals, or the operation of for-profit "business activities". This competition has led to a highly sophisticated fundraising industry within the voluntary sector in which larger and more established and recognized institutions (such as hospitals, universities and major health organizations) have a substantial edge over others in the sector;
- greater demands for accountability by governments, funders and the general public. Accountability is defined not only in terms of proper use of funds but in the effectiveness and efficiency of the organization and in meeting the needs of the community;
- more knowledgeable volunteers who have specific "wants" from their volunteer experiences;
- greater reliance on directors and a resulting increased concern about potential liability.

There are two conceptual approaches to "governance" and "stewardship". The more traditional approach is that the directors "manage" the affairs of the organization. The board would make most substantive decisions based on materials provided for board meetings and the discussion or debate at the meeting. The second approach is based on an "oversight" role for the directors to ensure that the organization is effective and is accountable. The oversight role relies more on the development of operational and other "policies" by the board of directors, which then looks to the officers and staff to implement.[5] The two approaches are sometimes labelled the "administrative governance board" model and the "policy governance board" model.

In reality, most organizations have operated and will continue to operate using a mixture of these two approaches. If the organization has staff, by-laws would, for example, often permit the executive director to manage staff in accordance with board-established human resource policies. Often, the by-laws or board resolutions determine the authority of the executive director to spend money within a budget set by the board. For larger organizations, these policies have typically included human resources, financial operations, advocacy, programming and so forth. Staff would be required to report to the board or a committee of the board on compliance with and deviation from the policies and on issues that arise for which greater direction is required.

There are both practical and legal limits to the extent to which boards may "delegate" their responsibilities through the issuance of policies. Boards will always have an "oversight" role in any organization but boards of corporations must be able to demonstrate that they "manage the affairs" of the corporation. Subsection 283(1) of the Ontario *Corporations Act*, for example, provides that the directors are to manage the affairs of the corporation.[6]

The proper mixture of "management" and "oversight" through policies is organization- and time-specific. There are practical limits to the abilities of directors to manage the affairs of large organizations with many employees. It is physically impossible for these directors to make all of the decisions that are required to be made on a day-to-day basis. Arguably, these directors could be negligent if they attempted to do so because decisions would not be made by the person most competent to do so, the decisions would not be made in a timely manner and the directors would be wasting the skills and talents of its employees. The same argument, however, could not be made for a small organization that has no employees and has no significant day-to-day activities. Although that organization may want policies in place to guide the board's

---

5 John Carver is a major proponent of this approach, which gained prominence with the publication of his *Boards that Make a Difference: A New Design for Leadership in Non-profit and Public Organizations* (San Francisco: Jossey-Bass Publications, 1991). Although not necessarily new conceptually, the text became an important opportunity for boards and organizations to re-examine how they operate and what structures were most appropriate for their circumstances. "Carverizing" an organization became a touchstone for some as a solution to many problems.

6 R.S.O. 1990, c. C.38.

decision-making, the board would continue to make most if not all decisions.

There is a spectrum between the two models of administrative governance and policy governance. Where on that spectrum an organization lays will depend upon a number of factors:

- the legal authority of the directors and officers and of the organization itself;
- statutory or common law obligations or restrictions;
- letters patent, by-laws, constitution or other constating documents;
- culture of organization;
- views and perspectives of key stakeholders;
- skills, competence and training of staff (assuming the organization has staff);
- size and type of operations and activities carried out by the organizations and their complexity; and
- due diligence requirements of the directors and of the officers.

There is no clear legal articulation of what is meant by "manage the affairs" of an organization. It will differ depending upon the issue, the circumstances and the organization. There are also certain decisions that are so fundamental to the affairs of any organization, that only the board should be making those decisions. For example, the budget of any organization ought to be approved by the directors and the board, or a committee of the board ought to be involved in the preparation of the budget for larger organizations. In other situations, the law may require that the board be involved other than through policy statements – either directly or indirectly where the ramifications are such that no prudent director would consent not to be involved.

The panel on governance and accountability recognized that there is no "one size fits all" approach to governance and stewardship. It recommended "a good practice guide for effective stewardship" for large and medium-sized organizations, which is also intended to be a checklist for smaller organizations. The panel concluded that there were eight tasks that were key to effective stewardship by boards:

1. *Mission and Strategic Planning*, which involves the definition of the fundamental goals and strategy of the organization. It considered this task the most important duty for the board because it established the basis for accountability — the basis on which to determine the appropriateness of the board's actions, performance of management

and the success of the organization. The mission and strategic planning, though, must be consistent with the letters patent and by-laws of the organization (or as they are amended in accordance with the law), any external restrictions on the use of the organization's assets, fiscal prudence and responsibility and any statutory, contractual or other legal obligations. Too often, organizations have developed very good mission statements and strategic plans — but ones that bear little if any relationship to what the organization can legally do.

For example, a church group incorporated for missionary purposes may not have the legal capacity to operate a summer camp, regardless of the usefulness of the summer camp.[7] If the letters patent establishing the corporation do not extend to this type of operation, the organization would be acting *ultra vires* or outside its legal capacity and the directors and officers could be personally liable for any damages to the corporation. These damages could include losses on the operations or from closing down the operation once it was determined that it could not operate the summer camp.

There are several components to the mission and strategic planning. The directors need to establish the mission, communicate it with the organization's members and stakeholders, and review it periodically to ensure that it is appropriate. A mission, if it is to be used to guide the organization's subsequent decision-making, will be an important statement and the board should consider the level and type of consultation it will undertake with the members, its employees, clientele, funders and the public. There ought to be a significant degree of up-front buy-in or comfort if the mission statement is to be accepted and become effective. The board also needs to develop strategic plans to implement the key elements of the mission statement; mission statements, like organizations themselves, can only become a reality to people being served through actions.

The board also needs to consider what the risks are and how to manage those risks. Any action involves risk and the board has a duty to anticipate risks, to understand those risks, to address them and to manage them. The board does not have a duty to avoid all

---

7 See for description of this example *Volunteers & the Law: A Guide for Volunteers, Organizations and Boards* (Vancouver: The People's Law School, 2000) at 54.

risks; the only way to do so would be to do nothing in life, which defeats the very purpose for the organization to exist.

The board needs to oversee and monitor the mission on a regular basis. It can do so by establishing measurable goals. The panel preferred "desired outcomes" or "impacts" over "inputs or activities" but it is not always clear how this can be accomplished. These goals are part of the tools of governance, which are discussed in another chapter.

2. *Transparency and Communication*, which help to ensure that the organization's activities are open and transparent and that there is communication between the organization and its members and stakeholders. This communication should be both ways. Openness and transparency, however, should not preclude appropriate confidentiality. For example, a board should not normally negotiate the purchase of a building in public, permitting the seller to know what the board's bottom line price is.

   Transparency and communication includes a number of elements. The board should establish policies for communication and feedback with stakeholders, a code of ethical conduct, and a complaints and grievance procedure that is effective. The board must meet regularly for discussion of matters and the making of decisions. Proper minutes and other documents must be kept to maintain the collective memory. Indeed, for corporations, the board has an obligation to do so and all organizations must do so under the *Income Tax Act*.[8] The organization should also respond appropriately to requests for information, recognizing that different requesters will have a different level of access to such information.

3. *Organizational Structures* should reflect the needs of the organization and its culture. Some organizations are part of a larger federation of organizations and its structure will likely be different from a stand-alone organization. Size and activities will also dictate differing structures. For example, a large organization may want an executive committee with decision-making powers. Care must be taken to ensure compliance with any legislative requirements or restrictions

---

[8] R.S.C. 1985 (5th Supp.), c. 1.

around committees. For example, if an executive committee is to be established, the Ontario *Corporations Act* has specific requirements that need to be in place. Furthermore, only an executive committee under that Act can make decisions; all other committees can at most be advisory.

The panel recommended that the structure reflect at least three elements: (i) that the board be capable of objective oversight, (ii) that there be an independent nominating committee to ensure appropriate succession of the board, and (iii) that an audit committee be established. The purpose of the audit committee would be to report on whether or not the organization is complying with the laws, rules, regulations and contracts that govern it and to review whether the management, information and control systems are organized and implemented to carry out these rules and regulations. The audit committee is also responsible for supervising external financial reporting. Whether there is one committee or more will be dependent on each organization.

This type of structure may not be appropriate for most organizations. The size of the organization and the scope of its operations may suggest a less sophisticated approach to organizational structure. Each organization needs to develop its own approach, and the more sophisticated approach may be more in keeping with a policy governance board model than one in which the board makes most of the decisions.

4. *Board's Understanding of Its Role* requires that the board members have a shared understanding of the role of the board and of the directors, officers and staff. An effective board is a major method to prevent problems from occurring and to address those when they do occur. The success or failure of an organization is dependent upon the board understanding its role and carrying out that role — however that role has developed in law or in practice. The effectiveness of a board of directors is discussed below.

5. *Fiscal Responsibility* is a cornerstone of accountability. This topic is reviewed in more detail later, but a number of matters should be highlighted. The board must ensure that the organization is in a financially sound position and that it has the resources necessary to

carry out its activities. If these two objectives are not possible, the board has two options from which to choose:

- locate and put in place the resources that are necessary; or
- alter the organization's programs to fit the resources that are available.

While any human activity — not-for-profit or for-profit — is not without risk, the board should not put the assets of the organization at unnecessary or unknown risk. Risk is part of life but the board needs to know and understand the likely risks and put in place the tools to minimize and manage those risks.

The directors have both statutory and common law duties towards the organization and often to third parties to ensure that the organization is operated in a financially prudent manner. These duties are sometimes referred to as some of the "fiduciary duties" of directors. The board, in fulfilling its duties, ought to put in place:

- a budget that is based on the mission and strategic plan of the organization and its priorities, consistent with its legal obligations and limitations, and on a realistic estimate of revenues and expenses;
- mechanisms to monitor and control expenditures. These mechanisms will normally include the accounting books and records that are required to be kept by law and by generally accepted accounting principles, financial statements (including audited statements where required) and reports on a regular basis. In the case of a registered charity, the *Income Tax Act* establishes certain requirements for record-keeping;
- tools to ensure that the assets of the organization are managed appropriately and consistently with the organization's legal obligations and that any liabilities do not become excessive or unmanageable.

Boards too often fail to devote the resources that are necessary to ensure that prudent financial practices occur. However, without the resources being available and properly managed, the organization cannot fulfil its objectives and the underlying purpose of the organization is not possible. Human nature being what it is, it is also to financial prudence that others look in making their decisions about an organization. Organizations that become insolvent or that have substantial losses due to defalcation or misuse of funds that could have been avoided are not trusted. The voluntary sector operates on the basis of "trust" — both trust in its legal sense and in its human sense.

6. *Oversight of Human Resources* is necessary because human resources are an important asset of the organization. Human resources includes staff and volunteers. The oversight of human resources requires the directors to ensure that the human resources have appropriate skills, training and backgrounds for the positions they occupy. Proper recruitment processes, job descriptions and performance appraisals are the responsibility of the directors — either directly or through management staff reporting to the directors. These processes ought to be fair and open.

   The board must also ensure that the organization complies with the various statutory schemes that are in place, including employment legislation, workplace safety, labour legislation, collective agreements, and human rights codes. There should be codes of conduct, including conflicts of interest. Appropriate screening processes should be in place for both staff and volunteers, especially where they deal with children, the elderly or vulnerable in the community.

7. *Assessment and Control Systems* are based in large measure on the accounting books and records. However, the systems often include codes of ethical conduct, an effective monitoring and complaints procedure, a framework for internal regulations (such as a constitution or by-laws), compliance audits and an evaluation of the board as a whole.

8. *Planning for Succession and Diversity* is important for organizations. In addition, organizations should reflect the diversity of the community in which they operate.

These concepts are not new but restated for a changing Canada. Others have articulated similar tasks in slightly different ways.[9] In one case, the author identified the following ten "responsibilities" of directors:[10]

- determine the mission;
- select the executive;
- support and evaluate the executive;
- lead planning;
- secure adequate resources;
- manage resources;
- set and monitor programmes;
- public relations;
- "court of appeal";
- self-assessment.

C EFFECTIVE BOARDS

In general, the board is responsible for overseeing the day-to-day operations of the organization. The directors have a duty to manage the organization — but they also have a duty to operate it, i.e., to ensure that it has activities that carry out its objects. It may do so through the development and implementation of policies and programs that meet the objectives of the organization. The directors are also responsible for ensuring that the organization complies with its common law and statutory obligations — which include those related to the area in which it operates (such as child care), employment law, environmental law, taxation and other statutory requirements.

The board is, however, made up of individuals. This fact is sometimes overlooked and individuals have differing views and personalities. One of the critical, practical roles of the board is to ensure that the board and the directors that comprise this human institution work in an effective and efficient manner — at the same time, recognizing and taking into account the different backgrounds, cultural and personal experiences, interests and personalities of the individuals.

---

9 See, for example, M.A. Paquet, R. Ralston & D. Cardinal, *A Handbook for Cultural Trusts* (Waterloo Ont.: University of Waterloo Press, 1987); and S. Kreiger, *Duties and Responsibilities of Directors of Non-Profit Corporations* (Toronto: Canadian Society of Association Executives, 1989).

10 R.T. Ingram, *Ten Responsibilities of Non-Profit Boards* (Washington: National Center for Nonprofit Boards, 1988).

There are several important "policies" or statements that should be in place so that existing and new directors understand what their roles are and what limits exist. These statements should first set out whether or not the board is to operate on the basis of "policy governance" or "administrative governance". The policy governance model gained favour in the 1990s. The board is intended to carry out its legal obligations by setting policies and monitoring the implementation by staff. Staff, in this model, are authorized to make decisions within the stated policies. An administrative governance model leaves decision-making with the board, which retains responsibility for implementation of its decisions. Obviously, the policy governance model is feasible only where there is staff — and staff that has the skills and training necessary to carry out the functions. It is more appropriate for larger, very sophisticated organizations and where the directors could not make and implement all the decisions.

Increasingly, boards are also establishing codes of conduct to ensure that directors understand their roles and that they behave in an appropriate manner. The codes may include a conflict of interest policy, or that policy may be separate. There may also be "job descriptions" for directors, which identify expectations of each director with respect to, for example, fundraising or public speaking. Just as with staff, it is a good idea to include criteria to assess board performance and how well a director carried out his or her duties.

The overall purpose of the board is to provide direction to the organization to permit it to carry out its objects, and to ensure that the organization meets its legal obligations (including maintenance of its status) and is financially responsible. The board must plan on how it intends to carry out the objects of the organization and to use the available resources to do so.

The board should allocate specific functions and tasks to specific positions, which are filled by individuals. Typically, the by-laws will do so for the president, vice-president, treasurer and secretary, and for larger organizations, for certain staff, such as the executive director. The individuals filling those positions are responsible to the board for their performance of the functions and tasks.

Boards often operate through committees, both standing and *ad hoc* committees. Care must be taken to ensure that any committees that are established comply with the governing law. For example, the Ontario *Corporations Act* permits the establishment of an executive committee with decision-making powers in certain circumstances but all other committees may be advisory only. The committees should each have terms of reference, even if they are functioning only in an advisory capacity.

The proper and respectful conduct of the board meetings is essential for the board to fulfil its obligations. If decisions are to be made by the board of directors — either to establish policies and monitor their implementation as a "policy governance board" or to make day-to-day decisions as an "administrative governance board" — there must be a controlled forum in which to make those decisions.

The affairs of the organization are transacted at meetings and those meetings should be run in an effective manner. There is no single rule on how to ensure that meetings are effective but a number of techniques may be highlighted:

- clarity of purpose of the organization — all in attendance should know and understand what the purpose of the organization is, its activities and the issues at hand. New directors should receive orientation so that they can contribute as soon as possible;
- clarity of purpose of the meeting — the purpose of the meeting, be it a regular monthly meeting or a special meeting, should be clear. A well drafted agenda will indicate the topics for discussion, for decision and for information, the priorities of the meeting and the allocated times. Background materials should be sufficient for the directors to understand the issues, to contribute to the meeting and to make any necessary decisions;
- clarity of the rules — rules or procedures are used to facilitate a meeting to allow it to be conducted smoothly and to avoid confusion and unfairness (actual or perceived). While strict enforcement of the rules should not stifle or kill debate, they should not be so loosely enforced that effective decision-making or debate is lost. The rules need to be clear, explicit and understood by all;
- unwritten rules — in most organizations, there are unwritten rules or norms that people take for granted. These have sometimes been developed to avoid conflict or to accommodate the specific needs of individuals. While these unwritten rules assist the board, newer directors may not be aware of them. A process should be in place to acquaint new directors with these unwritten rules — and other directors should be cognizant that it is very difficult for newer directors to know about an unwritten rule if it is not made known to them. In any event, the board should take care to ensure that any such unwritten rules are not in conflict with the law and the organization's by-laws and written rules;

- enjoyable meetings — individuals should find the meetings overall to be enjoyable, worthwhile and effective. This objective is true for any meeting but it is particularly important where the individuals are giving up their time for the public good. They want and deserve a level of personal satisfaction and enjoyment from the meetings — always within context of what their jobs are as a director. The sense of enjoyment may be enhanced by a better meeting place or modest amenities, such as refreshments;
- skills of the chair — effective meetings depend upon the skills of the chair. The chair needs to be in control of the meeting and have prepared for the meeting. A lack of preparation and ineffectiveness will have a negative impact on the meeting. The chair should be and be seen to be fair and even-handed in dealing with matters as they arise — including any personality conflicts that may occur. The chair needs to ensure that all directors have a fair opportunity to participate in the meeting and to avoid excessive or repetitive participation by a few. The skills necessary to chair a meeting are ones that are developed with experience and time and tolerance on the part of others.

Effective boards are possible.[11] They generally have in place mechanisms to assess the community need for the organization so that it remains relevant. At times, these mechanisms may reveal that the organization is no longer needed and that its resources could be better used elsewhere. However, more often the organization will identify a better way to operate in the community or to alter itself to meet the needs in a more effective manner. Sometimes, changes, to the organization's by-laws or letters patent or, more simply, to its policies will be needed. The board is responsible for undertaking such assessments on a periodic basis or as needed.

The board must also plan within the context of the organization's mission and strategic plans. These plans are used to state what activities the organization will carry out and what outcomes are expected, what tasks are to be done and by whom, and how these plans relate to the organization's objects and resources and the budgetary process. They are intended to ensure that the organization's priorities are being met, in accordance with its legal obligations. It is useful to identify options during

---

[11] See D. Abbey-Livingstone & B. Wiele, *Working with Volunteer Boards: How to Improve Their Effectiveness* (Toronto: Ontario Ministry of Citizenship and Ontario Association of Volunteer Bureaux/Centres, 1994).

the planning process and the pros and cons for each option so that the directors can determine which activities best meet and affect the organization's objects and resources.

The implementation of the plans involves the carrying out of the tasks identified in the plans and the ongoing coordination of the tasks. The board must be sensitive in implementing the plans should circumstances change. An unanticipated shortfall in revenues, for example, will require that the board either locate new resources, reallocate resources or amend the plan. The board should also evaluate plans and how they were implemented — both for purposes of accountability and monitoring, and to learn from what worked and what did not work. The evaluations will also assist in determining how relevant and effective the organization is in the community which it serves.

Boards should also manage relationships. They need to communicate internally and externally to stakeholders. Conflicts need to be managed so that they become productive outcomes or are resolved. If conflict is not managed, the board will have difficulty in developing and implementing plans and in carrying out the objects of the organization. Relationships with others outside the organization are equally important — be they regulators, governments, funders, corporate partners, clientele or the general public. Management of volunteers and their proper motivation is also part of the role of the board.

D DUE DILIGENCE

The first opportunity for a director to exercise due diligence is before he or she becomes a member of the board, either by election or by appointment. A potential director or officer should develop a good understanding of the organization and the area in which it operates before agreeing to be appointed or elected. For example, the individual should determine and understand:

- the objects and activities of the organization. These objects should be set out in the letters patent or similar document incorporating the organization, in the trust deed if the organization is a trust or in the other constating documents, such as a memorandum of association, if an unincorporated association. The activities would usually be identified in an annual report, strategic plan, report to funders, financial statements, brochures or similar document;
- the statutes, regulations and policies under which the organization operates. The first step is to review the incorporating legislation, if

the organization is a corporation. In addition, it is important to understand the legal framework that may exist for the organization, including taxation legislation, supervisory statutes and similar statutory regimes. These statutes will often set out or define obligations and thus areas for potential liability for the organization and for individual directors;

- the regulators who have jurisdiction over the organization. What are the formal and informal expectations of the regulators? Is the organization in compliance with the requirements? Has the organization completed its annual filings?
- financial position of the organization. This type of information is usually (or ought to be) available in the financial statements, reports to regulators (including Canada Customs and Revenue Agency) and to funders. There may be restrictions on the use of funds, either by statute, contract or internal decisions. In addition, the potential director would want to determine if there is any outstanding or potential litigation involving the organization, its directors or its officers for breach of contract, statute or other legal obligation.

Once the individual is a director, he or she must exercise due diligence in carrying out his or her fiduciary duties. Due diligence is both a question of fact and of law. What is due diligence will depend on the circumstances, the type of organization and the activities undertaken. In general, directors or officers will meet their obligations if they act reasonably, prudently and sagaciously and within the law, including the objects of the organization and the scope of their position or office. They should participate fully in the decisions of the organization. Participation means attending meetings and being prepared for those meetings by reviewing and understanding the materials and issues. Directors should also express their views and participate in the discussion of issues and information. Minutes of meetings should accurately reflect the discussion and the decisions.

The Ontario Public Guardian and Trustee has summarized the general duties of the directors of charities as follows:

> Directors and trustees must handle the charity's property with the care, skill and diligence that a prudent person would use. They must treat the charity's property the way a careful person would treat their own property. They must always protect

the charity's property from undue risk of loss and must ensure that no excessive administrative expenses are incurred.[12]

This summary is designed for directors and trustees of charities, but it is illustrative of the duties of directors of other organizations in the voluntary sector.

Directors of organizations that are not charitable but otherwise not-for-profit must also fulfil certain fiduciary duties. They owe duties to the organization, duties that are generally called "fiduciary duties". Fiduciary duties are a product of the common law, but there may also be specific duties that apply to directors as a result of statutory law. For example, directors may be liable for unpaid wages under incorporating legislation or for the payment of any unremitted taxes or employment-related premiums for employment insurance, Canada or Quebec Pension Plans, private pension plans and so forth.

Directors and officers of an organization must act with a reasonable degree of prudence, to be diligent, to act in good faith, honestly and loyally, and to avoid conflicts of interest. The courts have applied the common law duty of loyalty, for example, to corporate directors and officers. In *Canadian Aero Service Ltd. v. O'Malley*, Chief Justice Laskin concluded that a director, as a fiduciary, had a duty to act loyally, honestly, in good faith and to avoid personal profit.[13]

Liability does not turn on whether or not the director acted in bad faith; rather no fiduciary may "have an interest that possibly conflicts with the interests of those whom he is bound to protect", according to *Aberdeen Railway Co. v. Blaikie Bros.*[14] In *Regal (Hastings) Ltd. v. Gulliver*, the House of Lords decided that the test is whether or not the director has a personal conflict.[15] If there is a personal conflict, the director could be liable to account for any profits he or she made or will make. The rationale is that the director has a fiduciary relationship to the organization and out of that relationship the director made a profit.[16]

The Supreme Court of Canada took a similar approach in the *Canadian Aero* case. The court looked to the circumstances to determine whether or not a conflict existed. The types of factors that the court should consider included the:

---

12 *Charities Bulletin No. 3* – "Duties, Responsibilities and Powers of Directors and Trustees of Charities" (Toronto: Office of Public Guardian and Trustee, July 1999) at 2.

13 [1974] S.C.R. 592.

14 (1854), 2 Eq. Rep. 1281 (H.L.).

15 [1942] 1 All E.R. 378 (H.L.).

16 *Ibid.*, at 385.

> ... position or office held, the nature of the corporate opportunity, its ripeness, its specificness and the director's or managerial officer's relation to it, the amount of knowledge possessed, the circumstances in which it was obtained and whether it was special or, indeed, even private, the factor of time in the continuation of fiduciary duty where the alleged breach occurs after termination of the relationship with the company, and the circumstances under which the relationship was terminated, that is whether by retirement or resignation or discharge.[17]

These cases all involved for-profit corporations, however, the legal principles would appear to apply to directors and officers of organizations in the voluntary sector. They also apply regardless of the fact that directors would not receive payment for being a director of, for example, a charity.

Certain acts may be outside the legal capacity of the organization and, thus, of the directors. If the organization does not have the authority to carry out certain activities, the directors may be liable if they cause the organization to do so. In *Ashbury Railway Carriage & Iron Co. v. Riche*, the House of Lords held that if a contract was outside the scope of the corporation's power, it could not be ratified.[18] With few exceptions, most organizations in the voluntary sector are not considered legally to be "natural persons" and, as a result, care must be taken to ensure that the organizations do not act beyond their scope of power and authority. The directors are primarily responsible for doing so.

A related duty is the duty of care. The director must have the skills and competence to be a fiduciary. He or she must take care in making decisions but also bring to the position the required level of care and attention so that he or she understands the issues and makes appropriate decisions. There is

> a presumption that in making a business decision the directors of a corporation acted on an informed basis, in good faith and in the honest belief that the action taken was in the best interests of the company.[19]

The directors must exercise "vigilance, prudence and sagacity" and may be held personally liable if he or she is negligent by commission or omission.[20] The directors must also act in "good faith" at all times. "Good faith" is not easily defined but the director must have an honest belief

---

17 [1974] S.C.R. 592 at 620.

18 (1875), L.R. 7 H.L. 653 (H.L.).

19 *Aronson v. Lewis*, 473 A.2d 805 (Del. 1984) at 812.

20 *Fales v. Canada Permanent Trust Co.* (1976), [1977] 2 S.C.R. 302 at 318.

that what he or she is doing or proposes to do is proper and appropriate.[21] If not, the director may be held personally liable and accountable for any losses. The director is not, though, an insurer for the organizations. Loss alone is not sufficient to hold the director personally liable; rather there must be some evidence of wrongdoing or failure to exercise his or her duties.[22]

Directors also have a duty not to delegate if they are trustees or quasi-trustees, which is the case for charities. This issue has become particularly problematic with respect to investment decisions. The *Trustee Act*[23] and the common law do recognize certain practical matters which may be delegated. For example, section 20 of the *Trustee Act* permits the trustee to delegate to a solicitor as the organization's agent to receive and give a discharge for any money or valuable consideration or property receivable by the trustee under the trust.

Conflicts of interest provide the greatest difficulties for directors — whether acting as a trustee or quasi-trustee or as a director. In the case of trusts, the trustee may not benefit at all directly or indirectly unless the trust deed expressly permits or a court authorizes the trustee to do so. The organization should have in place a conflict of interest policy that at a minimum complies with the law and is reflective of the circumstances of the organization.

Directors of charities are held to a high standard. While directors of businesses or even not-for-profit organizations that are not charitable may enter into contracts with the organization, where appropriate disclosure has occurred,[24] directors of charities may not do so. They are also held to a different standard of care than are directors of business corporations. Most modern incorporation statutes establish a reasonable person test for directors. Unfortunately, most legislatures in Canada have not modernized incorporation statutes for not-for-profit and charitable corporations.

The standard of care in most Canadian jurisdictions is a subjective one. The subjective standard of care is a common law (as opposed to

---

21 Ontario Law Reform Commission, *Report on the Law of Trusts*, vol. 1 (Toronto: Ontario Ministry of Attorney General, 1984) at 24.

22 *Chapman Re, Cocks v. Chapman*, [1896] 2 Ch. 763 (C.A.) at 775.

23 R.S.O. 1990, c. T.23.

24 Section 71 of the Ontario *Corporations Act*, R.S.O. 1990, c. C.38, for example, permits a director of a not-for-profit corporation to disclose a direct or indirect interest in a contract or proposed contract. If the director complies with section 71, the director would not normally be accountable to the corporation.

statutory law)[25] development. The classic common law statement of the standard of care for directors is *City Equitable Fire Insurance Co., In re.*[26] in which the court concluded that the directors must exercise the degree of skill that "may reasonably be expected from a person of his knowledge and experience". This standard of care is subjective and means that a lawyer will be held to a higher standard than would a board member who has no legal training. Similarly, an individual with accounting or business experience would be held to a higher standard of care.

Directors are not limitless in their liability. Errors in business judgement, for example, would not automatically give rise to liability. The courts recognize that errors can occur, even by the most experienced and knowledgeable directors. The issue is whether or not the directors made the decision in a reasonably prudent manner as would be expected of a person with their knowledge and experience.

---

[25] In British Columbia, the *Society Act*, R.S.B.C. 1996, c. 433 establishes a standard of care that is more consistent with modern business incorporation statutes. Section 25 uses the test of "care, diligence and skill of a reasonably prudent person".

[26] [1925] 1 Ch. 407 (C.A.) at 428.

Chapter 2

TOOLS OF GOVERNANCE AND ACCOUNTABILITY

A INTRODUCTION

Directors and senior management of any organization — for profit or not-for-profit — are responsible for ensuring that the organization operates within the law and in a financially viable manner. There are a number of critical decisions that must be made by directors and senior management periodically and on a regular, day-to-day basis. These decisions involve the overall strategic direction of the organization, the planning to implement the strategic direction, obtaining the resources necessary to implement the strategic direction, and implementing that direction. Also important — but often overlooked — is the ongoing monitoring and assessment of the strategic direction or plans, and their implementation.

The duties and responsibilities on directors and senior management are high but there are a number of tools that may be used to assist them in fulfilling their obligations. In some cases, these tools are mandated by legislation or by the common law. For example, financial books and records must be maintained by organizations pursuant to incorporating legislation,[1] taxation legislation[2] (even if the organization is exempt from paying taxes, it may be obliged to maintain appropriate books and records) and, in the case of trustees, by the common law and in Ontario the *Charities Accounting Act*[3] and the *Trustee Act*.[4]

The tools are, however, just that — tools. The directors and senior management must exercise good judgement in developing the strategic

---

1 See, for example, s. 117 of the *Canada Corporations Act*, R.S.C. 1970, c. C-32 and s. 302 of the Ontario *Corporations Act*, R.S.O. 1990, c. C.38.

2 *Income Tax Act*, R.S.C. 1985 (5th Supp.), c.1.

3 R.S.O. 1990, c. C.10.

4 R.S.O. 1990, c. T.23.

direction and plans for the organization, and in implementing them. The direction and plans ought to be ones that make sense in context of the organization's background, its strengths, weaknesses, opportunities and threats (sometimes called "SWOT") and the needs of its community. For example, an organization that has no or few staff or volunteers probably should not set as its strategic direction the operation of a significant facility or program that requires substantial and skilled human resources — or if it does, to put in place detailed plans to do so.

Directors and senior management, in order to fulfil their obligations, need to know about the organization and its financial and operational situation. They need to have a good understanding, therefore, of the relevant tools. The level of knowledge and understanding will vary depending upon whether the individual is a director, an officer or senior manager. For example, the treasurer will be expected to have a much more thorough knowledge and understanding of financial statements, books of account and so forth than will a "director-at-large". However, that director should be able to "read" financial statements and to understand what is being said in those statements, *e.g.*, is the organization financially solvent or insolvent? Is the cash flow adequate? Or will the organization need to obtain a line of credit? Does the organization have the resources to carry out its activities? Or is some trimming required?

This chapter will examine the basic tools that are used as part of the governance of an organization and its accountability. It will look at the strategic planning, long term planning and operational planning processes, including budgeting. Financial information and the presentation of this information is critical to planning and to accountability and, as a result, is discussed at some length. But first, the chapter reviews the Panel of Accountability and Governance in the Voluntary Sector's model for effective stewardship. The overall discussion is continued in Chapter 3, which is concerned with the next stage of stewardship — managing risk.

B PANEL ON ACCOUNTABILITY AND GOVERNANCE IN THE VOLUNTARY SECTOR — NEW STANDARDS FOR A NEW ERA

I. Introduction

The Panel on Accountability and Governance in the Voluntary Sector was a major initiative of several larger charitable organizations in Canada. The Panel was comprised of highly regarded Canadians who undertook a broad consultation in the sector on accountability and governance. The Panel made a number of recommendations, which have become the basis for ongoing discussion in the sector and with government.[5]

These recommendations have led to a multi-year "reform" initiative between the Government of Canada and the sector. *Working Together: A Government of Canada/Voluntary Sector Joint Initiative*[6] was the first major product of this joint effort. However, it is expected that the end result will include a higher standard of accountability in and for the sector.

The Panel's recommendations, therefore, have become seminal for the sector, especially as they deal with two major areas for which directors and senior management have responsibilities — accountability and governance. The recommendations were generally intended to improve effective stewardship in the sector, while recognizing that the standards will be different depending upon the size of the organizations. The standards and requirements for a large, interprovincial charitable organization will, by necessity, be different from those for a local neighbourhood association. The need for honesty, integrity, accountability and transparency remain the same; but inevitably how these objectives are implemented will vary from organization to organization.

The Panel made a number of specific recommendations, which form the background for accountability and governance for an organization. The Panel was also very clear — it is the responsibility of the board of directors to carry out the appropriate analysis and to put in place the relevant elements of "effective stewardship". The recommendations were grouped around twelve areas, each of which are reviewed below. Together, these recommendations are the Panel's "guidelines" that are intended to increase the effectiveness of the board's stewardship. Given the credibility of the Panel and its work, the extensive consultation and the ongoing work arising from it, the recommendations are likely to be reflected in the law, in standards or as "best practices".

II. Mission and Strategic Planning

The Panel considered this area to be the most important duty of the board. Essentially, the board is to define the fundamental goals and strategy for the organization. Without doing so, the board has no basis to

---

5 *Building on Strength: Improving Governance and Accountability in Canada's Voluntary Sector*, Final Report (Ottawa: February 1999).

6 Report of the Joint Tables (August 1999).

assess whether or not its actions are appropriate or to assess the performance of management or the success of the organization.

Mission and strategic planning require that the board do several things:

- the board should establish the mission for the organization and communicate that mission with the organization's members and stakeholders. It should also periodically review the appropriateness of that mission. The board, as part of its duties, ought to identify key elements to success, which would include sustaining the mission and establishing a strategic planning process to reach the mission. The process for establishing a mission and strategic planning is discussed below;
- it should approve a process for risk assessment and management. The purpose of doing so is to assist the board in anticipating risk, assessing it, and managing the outcome of risky actions. Risk assessment and management is discussed more fully in Chapter 3;
- oversee and monitor the achievement of the mission by setting measurable goals, defined in terms of desired outcomes or impacts on clients, rather than as inputs or activities. This recommendation is reviewed below.

III. Transparency and Communication

The Panel makes several recommendations with respect to transparency and communication — with the public, with the members and with the organization's constituencies. "Transparency and communication" for the Panel requires that the board:

- establish policies for communicating and receiving feedback from stakeholders;
- ensure the complaints and grievance procedure works effectively. This procedure is to be established as part of a code of ethical conduct;
- hold regular board meetings that provide an opportunity for discussion;
- provide a collective memory of the organization by ensuring that appropriate minutes and documents are kept;
- respond appropriately to requests for information.

Several of these requirements have a legal component. For example, the maintenance of minutes and other similar documents is required by incorporating legislation and taxation legislation. Trustees must also maintain such records in order to fulfil their common law duties as trustees. This area is reviewed in more detail in Chapter 3.

IV. Structures

Structures are important for the Panel and, therefore, for the board of directors. The structure of an organization will affect how it operates and its efficiency and effectiveness. There is no single "structure" that is appropriate to all organization; furthermore, an organization's structure may change over time as it develops or reacts to altering circumstances.

The Panel recommends that an organization have three basic elements if the board is to provide independent oversight and effective stewardship:

- a board capable of providing objective oversight;
- an independent nominating committee to ensure the appropriate succession of the board; and
- an audit committee, whose primary responsibility is to report whether the organization is in compliance with the laws, rules, regulations and contracts that govern it. It reviews whether the management, information and control systems are organized and implemented to carry out these rules and regulations, and as well is responsible for supervising external financial reporting.

The latter two recommendations may not always be relevant, notwithstanding the position taken by the Panel. For example, the culture of the organization and its history will more often than not dictate how "succession" occurs. The Panel itself recognized that church-based organizations have special requirements, which may override its own recommendations. Also, some organizations have various affiliations or overarching structures that preclude compliance with these recommendations. Finally, these recommendations seem more appropriate for boards that are "policy" oriented as opposed to those boards that are active or "administrative" in nature. Tangential to this point, some organizations have a very active membership that participates in regular meetings at which decisions are made.

In any event, the underlying theme raised by the Panel is important, in particular for organizations that are medium to large and have staff to implement plans. These types of organizations will tend to have boards of directors that are not as active in the day-to-day activity of the organization and, therefore, must provide that independent oversight on behalf of the membership and, to some extent, the public and regulators.

V. Board's Understanding of Its Own Role

The board's understanding of its own role is critical to effective stewardship. If the board as a collective and as individual directors is not aware of the proper role (as is appropriate for that organization), effective stewardship is not likely to be achieved. The board should have a shared understanding of this role to avoid dissonance, disharmony, disjointedness or delays. Boards should:

- decide upon and communicate their philosophy of governance. The two basic types of governance are: (i) "policy governance" where the board makes policy and provides strategic direction, but takes a hands off approach towards day-to-day management, and (ii) "administrative governance", where the board not only sets policy but does some of the implementation itself. Larger organizations generally prefer the policy governance approach but this approach requires staff with a high level of skills and knowledge;
- develop a code of conduct for board members to help directors understand and ensure they agree to the obligations which they are undertaking;
- establish and enforce a written conflict of interest policy governing board members and staff or volunteers who have independent decision-making authority over the resources of the organization;
- provide job descriptions for board members that outline general duties and how the board's work will be evaluated;
- invest in board orientation and ongoing information sessions;
- recognize contributions of board members and provide feedback on the board's performance;
- use the time of the board members effectively.

These specific recommendations are discussed in Chapter 3 in more detail. They are generally part of the risk management approach that boards ought to undertake.

VI. Fiscal Responsibility

Fiscal responsibility is, of course, essential and one of the major legal obligations of boards. For many, fiscal responsibility is a simple matter — do not spend more than you earn. However, fiscal responsibility can be and often is more complicated than that simple statement. Certainly, it is important that the organization maintain (or become) financially solvent. But the context and purpose for charitable and not-for-profit organizations must be kept in mind. These organizations are created to carry out their objects, not to sit on their assets. Fiscal responsibility includes a recognition of the social benefits that flow from the objects of the organization and the implementation of those objects.

What is important for directors is to ensure that they meet their fiduciary and other legal obligations with respect to the organization. A failure to do so can lead to personal liability. In general, the board must:

- approve a budget that reflects the organization's priorities and is based on realistic assumptions of revenues, costs and other factors such as inflation;
- monitor and control expenditures, based on appropriate accounting procedures;
- oversee stewardship of organization assets and liabilities;
- oversee the issuance and record-keeping of receipts for charitable donations, if a registered charity;
- approve annual reports, including financial statements.

These activities are discussed below and in Chapter 3.

VII. Human Resources — Employees and Volunteers

Oversight of human resources is another important function of the board. Human resources, in this context, includes both employees and volunteers. Volunteers are particularly important in this sector, given that a significant portion of charitable and not-for-profit organizations have no or few staff.

In the case of employees, the board should:

- ensure that the organization complies with employment legislation and workplace safety regulations, and reviews its employment arrangements periodically to ensure they comply with good practice;

- ensure staff are provided with job descriptions, orientation, management, training and performance appraisals;
- recruit staff openly, fairly and systematically;
- review periodically the staff structure and effectiveness of working relationship between the board and staff.

Volunteers ought to be dealt with in a similar manner, but one that recognizes the unique nature of volunteers. The board ought to:

- have a clear set of policies regarding recruitment, preparation, oversight and recognition of volunteers, and programs should be designed and assessed with the same stringency as other programs;
- give volunteers a clear statement of the tasks and activities that they are to carry out, perhaps with job descriptions or volunteer agreements;
- adopt and adhere to codes of ethical conduct for managers of volunteers and volunteers;
- provide adequate orientation, training and evaluation;
- publicly recognize the contribution of volunteers;
- screen volunteers, particularly if the organization works with vulnerable populations;
- provide direction and, in unionized environments, work with the unions to reach agreement on how the paid or non-voluntary volunteers are to be integrated into the organization;
- establish explicit expectations about the claiming of expenses.

Much of the board's role in this area is related to risk management. The risks may be to the organization directly or indirectly, or through the provision of services to the vulnerable. Chapter 3 focusses on risk management and this area will be reviewed in that chapter.

VIII. Assessment and Control Systems

Another key area for boards is assessment and control systems, especially for boards that have adopted the "policy governance" approach. However, all boards ought to put in place relevant and appropriate systems for assessment and control. These "systems" may be sophisticated or simple, depending upon the nature of the organization and the types of risks that are involved.

Typically, the Panel recommends that the board put in place:

- a code of ethical conduct and an effective monitoring and compliance procedure;
- a framework for internal regulations, including a constitution and by-laws (which might be quite simple in small organizations);
- a compliance audit as an integral part of the annual evaluation cycle to check that the rules governing the organization are being followed and that control systems are functioning and adequate (normally supervised by the audit committee of the board. Responsibility is to respond, indicating how the board has addressed issues of noncompliance identified by the committee);
- evaluation of the performance of the board as a collective.

These recommendations are more readily implemented in full in larger and more sophisticated organizations. It is not as easy to see, for example, a process to evaluate the performance of the board collectively if the organization is a neighbourhood association. However, the principles identified by the Panel are relevant to all organizations, regardless of size or activities. Different approaches may be needed to meet the principles.

IX. Succession Planning and Diversity

Succession planning and the encouragement of diversity is another role for boards. The Panel views this area as necessary to maintain the viability and health of an organization. The board must, therefore, plan for its own succession and recruit new directors. The Panel suggests that a nominating committee be appointed — one that is independent of management — to assess the qualities needed for the board, to develop selection criteria and to propose suitable candidates. The nominating committee must provide accurate and sufficient information to prospective candidates to allow them to understand the role and to make an informed decision.

The nominating committee — and the board as a whole — needs to reflect on the diversity of the board. Does it reflect the organization's constituencies? Community? The Panel notes that issues of diversity play out differently in organizations. The Panel is emphatic that it is not recommending a legislated approach. Rather, it suggests that a "good practice" would be for the board to discuss if representation of users and constituencies on the board is important to the organization's mission and credibility. If it is, then the board should work toward increasing diversity, ensuring representation is not token.

X. Reporting on Good Governance

Public reporting on good governance is one of the end-products of governance and accountability. A number of stakeholders have an interest in knowing how organizations govern themselves. The Panel recommends, as a base for all charities, that there be transparency, the avoidance of conflicts, and some reporting of activities and finances.

It recognizes that capacities will vary among organizations. But all organizations that issue receipts for income tax purposes ought to:

- provide certain information to the federal government about its governance, programs and finances;
- adhere to a code of ethical fundraising, such as the Canadian Centre for Philanthropy's or similar that is publicly available;
- practice transparency — respond appropriately to complaints and requests for information by the public, members or clients.

However, although not recommended by the Panel, it would seem appropriate that all organizations in the sector have similar information available to demonstrate accountability and good governance. While a small not-for-profit organization may not have any legal obligation to report under the *Income Tax Act* on its income and its activities, the boards of those organizations certainly ought to be in a position to do so. They need that information in a useable manner in order to carry out their obligations.

The Panel, in recognition of the varying capacities of organizations, made two sets of recommendations depending upon size of the organization:

- Required Reporting: The Basics
    - description of organization's mission, programs and intended results;
    - financial statements, as approved by the board;
    - description of fundraising activities over the past year including amount of revenues and amount spent raising them;
    - description of basic governance structures, including board size and methods for selecting board members;
    - disclosure of the code of ethical fundraising to which the organization adheres;

  - description of the organization's approach to responding to complaints;
  - how to get further information directly from the organization.

- Requirements for Larger Organizations

  - the nature of the mission, intended outcomes and strategic planning processes;
  - overview of policies for transparency, code of ethical conduct, complaints process, number of board meetings per year;
  - description of governing structures, including whether an independent nominating committee and an audit committee exist;
  - summary of the methods of board stewardship;
  - evidence of fiscal responsibility, as through provision of audited financial statements;
  - methods for board succession and diversity of representation, if applicable.

The Panel's recommendations are tied to the reporting requirements of charities under the *Income Tax Act*. These recommendations were directed more to the government to suggest what ought to be required (and currently is for registered charities). However, it also recommended that the method of reporting be more user friendly. Nevertheless, the recommendations illustrate the type of information that the Panel felt ought to be available in order to demonstrate both accountability and good governance.

C. PLANNING — THE STRATEGIC DIRECTION, LONG TERM PLANS, OPERATIONAL PLANS, BUDGETING AND ASSESSMENTS

I. Introduction

Strategic planning is not new to most people — in their personal, business or community lives. It is essentially determining where the directors, members and community want to take an organization over a specified period of time and how to get there. A strategic plan may cover a period of one year, two years, five years or another time period. The length of time is one of the elements of the strategic plan. It should reflect a realistic assessment of what can be done, taking into account that a community changes, an organization changes and its circumstances change. A strategic plan may be next to perfect for a couple of years, but cut-backs in funding may cause the organization to reassess that perfect strategic plan.

Planning has not been a strong element in the history of many organizations. Planning has a reputation for not being "fun" and individuals volunteer to be directors or to work for an organization in part to have "fun". Planning, if done properly, forces people to think, to analyse and to make choices. But without a plan, it is very difficult to demonstrate where the organization is going and what it wants to do. Without a plan, becoming more efficient and effective will be very difficult. Without a plan, determining what resources are necessary is next to impossible. Without a plan, how does an organization know when it has succeeded?

Proper planning is one of the tools that are available to boards of directors and senior management to address a problem identified by the Panel on Accountability and Governance in the Voluntary Sector. The Panel noted that:

> Where problems of organizational governance exist in the sector, they are due largely to the nature of volunteer boards, who often have limited time to devote to the task, are poorly informed about the nature of their responsibilities in the first place, or do not have access to the right tools to improve their own performance.[7]

The Panel's report continued that these problems may be compounded if they are combined with pressures of rising demands and fewer resources. The organization is forced to focus on the day-to-day tasks and cannot step back to evaluate itself and to make changes. However, it must do so if it is to adapt, to be accountable and to be efficient and effective.

The directors and senior management may simply be regurgitating old plans and budgets, without sufficient analysis or thought. This approach detracts from the overall effectiveness and accountability of an organization. It also can lead to financial problems — ones that creep up on the organization and its directors and senior management because of lack of attention to detail and planning.

There are many different approaches to strategic planning and overall planning and almost as many different terms for the elements of the plans

---

7 *Building on Strength: Improving Governance and Accountability in Canada's Voluntary Sector*, Final Report (Ottawa: February 1999) at 21.

and the processes.[8] In general, however, there is a consensus that planning involves the development through an iterative process with several phases.

II. Mission Statement

This element is an articulation of what the overall purpose and/or vision is of the organization. Obviously, the underlying basis for any mission statement or mission plan must be within the "objects" or "purposes" set out in the organization's incorporation documents (letters patent, articles or similarly named document depending upon the jurisdiction in which the organization is incorporated), constitution or memorandum of association (if not incorporated), or trust deed (for a trust).

The mission statement must fall within those objects and purposes. Some organizations have attempted to adapt to new circumstances by simply redefining themselves through a new mission statement — at times, a mission statement that is substantially different from what its incorporating documents permit the organization to do. The directors could be held personally liable in those situations because they are causing the organization to act outside (or *ultra vires*) what it is permitted to do by its own organizational documents.

It is important, therefore, for the mission statement to be consistent with and fall within the organization's legally defined objects and purposes. A mission statement could emphasize one or more of the objects over other objects (subject, of course, to any other legal obligations on the organization, such as a contract to provide certain services). But it should not propose that the organization carry out activities that are *ultra vires*. However, if the directors and members are of the view that, after the planning process has been undertaken, the objects are no longer reflective of the needs of the community or more appropriate opportunities are available to the organization but are outside its objects, the directors could propose to amend the objects. There may be legal requirements and restrictions in doing so, especially where the organization is a "trust", charitable or otherwise. But this approach is

---

8 One very useful approach is discussed in *A Handbook for Cultural Trustees: A Guide to the Role, Responsibilities and Functions of Boards of Trustees of Cultural Organizations in Canada* (Waterloo, Ont.: University of Waterloo Press, 1987) by M.A. Paquet with R. Ralston and D. Cardinal. Although intended for cultural organizations, the approach taken is equally applicable to most other types of charitable and not-for-profit organizations.

legally safer than ignoring the legally-provided-for objects and carrying on without regard to those objects.

Generally, mission statements are short in verbiage, but long in meaning. The board of directors may seldom see such "disputes" as it will over a few words. A lot is packed into and is intended to be packed into 30 or 40 words. Each word will have behind it much thought, emotion and resonance. And it should. The words, together, after all, define what the organization is about and what it hopes to be.

Each organization will go through its own process or processes. If there are employees or volunteers many organizations involve those employees or volunteers in the process. The members are also often involved if the organization is essentially "membership-based". Clients are sometimes consulted, especially where the organization provides goods or services to clients. And, of course, senior management and the directors need to be involved. While overall agreement may be difficult to obtain, there should be at the very least a significant degree of consensus with the mission statement if it is to be attainable.

Some groups will hire a consultant or facilitator to assist in developing the process for drafting the mission statement or in the actual drafting of the mission statement. The decision to do so ought to be made by the board. The board needs to be satisfied that the use of a consultant will add value to either the process or the end product given the costs. One of the advantages of retaining a consultant or facilitator is that he or she usually comes from outside the organization; they will not be personally hampered by the residue of past disputes, problems or personality conflicts. The consultant can become "an honest broker" or somebody who can reframe the issues in a more helpful manner. Another advantage is that they ought to be experts in this area and will be able to draw on previous experiences and knowledge to help the organization. The disadvantages include the costs, potential time delay (although the time normally should be made available for such an important matter) and lack of understanding of the organization. In addition, in some cases, the consultant may be driving a particular approach or result that is not appropriate for the organization.

III. Long Term Planning

Long term planning is intended to take the mission statement and provide guidance and direction on how to implement that mission statement. How long is a long term plan? There is no firm period. It should reflect the intentions set out in the mission statement and flow from that statement. Often, a long term plan covers a few years, in order to permit the development of programs or the obtaining of the resources necessary to achieve the plan's objectives. Typically, though, a plan will not exceed five years. Too much can change over a five-year period. Indeed, after five years, it may be time to reassess the mission statement — not necessarily to change it, but at least to examine it to see if it is still relevant.

Long term planning will start with the question of "where are we now"? The directors and senior management need to take a very critical approach to answering this question. What are the strengths? What are the weaknesses? What are the opportunities? What are the threats? What do we anticipate the future will (realistically) be? Do we have the resources (human, financial, organizational, physical) that are needed to achieve our goals? What resources will be needed to do so?

A long term plan will have specific goals and objectives that are to be achieved during its currency. These goals and objectives will normally be expressed along major areas of activities — for example, financial, fundraising, human resources, advocacy, communications, volunteer development, assessment and controls, programs, board development. Specific goals will be set out which will assist in marking progress in achieving the long term plan.

IV. Short Term Planning

Short term planning is sometimes called operational planning and will cover a one-year time period (or less). It is a portion of the longer term plan and will, of course be an attempt to attain the goals set out in that long term plan. The short term plan ought to reflect the mission statement and to assist in achieving that mission. Staff, if the organization has staff, will use the mission statement and the long term plan to develop the short term or operational plan. The operational plan will typically include objectives for the organization's different programs, the operating budget, fundraising plans, and so forth. The plans may include staff development, board development, communication, advocacy, legal plan (e.g., amendments to letters patent necessary to implement the mission statement) and so forth. The goals and objectives will be more specific and dollars and cents can be more readily attached to each goal and objective.

These plans will often be developed by staff or a committee of the board. The whole board, however, should approve of the plans — after appropriate discussion and amendments. Everybody needs to feel a sense of ownership over the plans. The level of consultations with others, such as employees, members or clients, though, will normally be minimal or not at all. The input from the members and clients, in particular, occurred as part of the mission statement development and, possibly, in the long term plans. However, the culture of an organization may dictate a higher level of involvement.

Unless there are other dynamics or legal requirements, the development and approval of short term plans is a function of senior management and the directors. There may be circumstances in which others need to be involved. For example, if the organization is providing services to the public, it is not uncommon for the contract with a government to require the approval of that level of government of the budget. There may also be good political reasons to review the short term plans (and their components) with others to ensure acceptance and buy-in. For example, some organizations will have public meetings to allow the general public to have input into the process.

V. Budgets

Budgets and their preparation is where the "rubber hits the asphalt" for any organization. The board may have undertaken a thorough mission statement development process, involving all of the stakeholders, and established long term plans from that mission statement. But the preparation of budgets is the process where real choices must be made in the allocation of resources to meet the objectives of the mission statement and plans.

A budget is a statement of an organization's anticipated revenues and expenditures for a specified fiscal period, usually a year. It should contain a description of the organization's activities and projects from three perspectives — budgeting, cash flow and budgetary control.

The budget fulfils at least three important functions for an organization. It should be used:

- to determine the resources needed to achieve the objectives for the fiscal period;
- to obtain approval from the board or membership and, if required, from external parties, for the programs and activities and use of resources; and
- to provide the basis for budgetary control and comparison.

The budget assists the organization in planning for both long and short term goals. It provides the board with a tool to control expenditures and to ensure that expenditures remain within the budget or that variances are explained. The budget may also be used as a yardstick against which results may be measured and in determining whether or not the benefits gained are adequate and worth the associated costs.

The budget is not only directly but also indirectly useful to the organization. Financial institutions will use the budget to make decisions on whether or not to loan the organization money or to make available a line of credit. Similarly, governments and other funders will usually require a budget to make funding decisions to ensure that the funding and the level of allocation are appropriate and that the organization will be accountable for the monies. A budget may also be used to keep the members informed and to provide information to the public as part of a fundraising campaign. For whatever reasons, people like to see numbers laid out in an understandable fashion and budgets seem to meet that need.

The budgetary cycle and its complexity largely depends upon the size, sophistication and purpose of the charitable or not-for-profit organization. A number of steps, however, are appropriate for most, if not all, organizations:

- a timetable for the preparation of the budget, which will ensure that the budget is drafted and approved in a timely manner;
- an examination of the objectives and activities for the budgetary period to determine if they are appropriate, desirable and achievable. There may be other factors to consider, such as the availability of staff or volunteers to carry out the activities. If they are not available or cannot be made available, that fact could mean that the budget would not include funding for that activity;
- a forecast of anticipated revenues and expenditures;
- the drafting of the budget;
- the review and approval of the draft budget by the board, the membership (if appropriate) or external stakeholders (if required);
- an ongoing comparison of the budget to actual results and reports during the fiscal period.

The budget should be related to the objectives of the organization for that fiscal period and should be realistic. A good budget will be a source of information on objectives and activities of the organization in addition to being a breakdown of anticipated revenues and expenditures. The budget must be realistic, not unattainable.

The sources of anticipated revenues would typically include membership fees, income from activities, interest income, sales of goods and services, bequests, donations, fundraising events, grants and similar monies or in-kind contributions. Anticipated expenditures vary from organization to organization and reflect the objects and activities of the organization. Expenditures will often include salaries, wages and benefits if there are staff, office expenses (postage, bank charges, stationery and so forth), rent or mortgage payments, insurance, property taxes, meeting expenses, professional fees (legal and accounting) and any capital expenditures.

The recognition of revenues and expenditures is an important part of budgeting. For example, if a contribution is restricted to a particular program or activity, those funds could also be used for that program or activity. The budget should recognize this restriction. The use of restricted and deferred funds is discussed in more detail later in this chapter.

Cash flow is an important part of budgeting. Aside from issues around the use of restricted or deferred funds, it is common for any organization to have cash coming in and going out at different rates and different times during the fiscal period. A cash flow analysis will assist in making sure that the cash is present when it is needed; if it is not going to be, the directors will need to make appropriate arrangements to defer the expenditure or payment of it, or for a loan or line of credit.

Certain information should be included in the cash flow analysis, including:

- when the money must be paid out;
- to whom the money is to be paid; and
- how much money is to be paid in and when.

This analysis tells the organization whether it has sufficient funds to pay accounts as they become due and allows the organization to make appropriate adjustments. In a worst-case situation, an otherwise viable organization will not be able to make its payments when they become due and could be considered to be insolvent or bankrupt. This situation is one to avoid.

There are some legal issues around loans. In Ontario, for example, charities may borrow money only for operational expenses, unless the money is borrowed on the security of real or personal property. The letters patent for any charitable or not-for-profit corporation should also be reviewed to ensure that there are no limitations or prohibitions. In some cases, the by-laws, trust deed or other constating document or resolutions may also place limits. Contractual relationships should also be reviewed to ensure that a loan will not result in default on the contract, including any pre-existing loan agreements. Finally, it may be important to ensure that certain assets are not included as collateral. For example, the directors will want to be careful about pledging as collateral any endowment funds or funds that are externally restricted for, say, a future building, if the loan is for operating expenses.

The budget allows an organization to control its activities. Budgetary control permits resources to be allocated in a rational and timely fashion. The approval process ensures commitment to the plan by all persons involved. Variances from the approved budget should be approved, either by the board or senior management, depending upon the governance structure being used by the organization. Variances ought to be analysed to determine whether or not the organization should change its procedures, plans or activities. If one activity is consistently over or under budget, it may be that that activity ought to undergo a more thorough review as part of the next budgetary cycle.

VI. Assessment and Evaluation

The Panel commented that "stated simply, the ultimate goal of accountability is to demonstrate that an organization does good in a good way."[9] Essentially, the organization should be able to show that it is effective and that the expenditures and privileges provided to charitable and not-for-profit organizations are worthwhile. One method to do so is an "outcome-based assessment", which is recommended by the Panel.

Outcome-based assessment is a tool for accountability and for planning. The underlying purpose is to encourage organizations to measure effectiveness through results and outcomes. Historically, organizations have (if at all) measured effectiveness through an examination of the activities and the inputs or outputs. For the Panel, there is a shift from how a program operates to the good it accomplishes.

The Panel recognized that this approach will be a difficult one for the sector. It noted that "while the intuitive logic in this shift is appealing, its implementation is more complex, and has posed a considerable challenge

---

9 *Building on Strength*, at 29.

to the voluntary sector in Canada, as elsewhere".[10] Nonetheless, the Panel encouraged organizations to adopt outcome-based assessment where possible.

Outcome-based assessment involves three activities, all of which are useful to do regardless of whether or not the organization adopts the overall approach suggested by the Panel. These activities are:

- identify outcome goals — this activity is likely the most difficult one, because it means the directors must establish specific and measurable goals that the organization is to achieve. But these goals are not in the nature of "120 clients referred to home services", the more traditional approach. Rather the goal should identify a final outcome for the services provided and how it affected the clients. Logically, the goals should also be tied into the organization's mission statement and to its long term plan.
- developing measures and collecting data — goals, in order to be effective, need to be measured against something. If there is nothing against which to measure the success of attaining the goal, it is not a useful goal. The Panel suggested the benchmark approach, i.e., determining what the benchmark is when the goal is established and what the goal is over a time period. This approach, of course, assumes that there is a benchmark against which to set a goal. It also assumes that the data can be readily collected in a useable form and cost effective manner.
- disseminating the results to stakeholders and using for planning purposes — the reason to implement outcome-based assessments is to demonstrate accountability and to use the information to become more effective and to meet the needs of the community. Obviously, the information needs to be in a user-friendly format to encourage its use.

Outcome-based assessment is one tool of accountability and planning. However, it is one that is, admittedly even by its proponents, difficult to implement. It may require a substantial investment to develop the outcome goals, to establish the measures and to collect the data. However, it may be appropriate for organizations — at least as part of its overall self-assessment and evaluation.

---

[10] *Ibid.*

There are more traditional approaches to assessment and evaluation. Of course, the first one is to determine at the end of the fiscal period whether or not the organization was on budget. Did it meet its stated objectives? If so, arguably, it was successful. If not, the directors need to find out why and to determine what can be done to correct the situation for the next period. In doing so, the directors ought not to ignore an obvious approach that is often overlooked — is the organization in the right business? Or should there be some fundamental changes to how it operates? Is it still meeting the needs of the community that it serves? Or has the community and its needs changed? Perhaps, even, it is time to re-examine the mission statement or long term plan for the organization.

The common approach to doing so is operational reviews.[11] An operational review lets an organization examine itself in an orderly manner. The purpose is to determine "what is" as the basis for change. It analyses and assesses the efficiency and effectiveness of an organization and identifies steps that can be taken to improve it. An operational review can be an involved process or a simple one. Whatever the details of the process, the organization will determine how well it uses its resources (human, financial and assets) to provide programs or activities to meet its goals and objectives.

The timing of an operational review will often dictate the process to be used. For example, if the organization, as part of its overall processes, wants to assess its "fitness", there will be a regular checklist. It is intended to identify problems early on and to provide solutions. The fitness approach can be used either in a management process or for a specific operational review. Both are cyclical in nature. The management process will begin with the establishment of objectives, the identification of priorities, the allocation of resources, the motivation to achieve the objectives and the evaluation. In an operational review process, there will be a problem identified, its cause defined, the development of options, the selection and implementation of the best option and the evaluation of whether or not the problem has been resolved.

Organizations will, however, occasionally be in crisis. The crisis approach is not dissimilar to the operational review which is undertaken as part of the normal planning cycle. However, it tends to be more poignant and the timing is shorter. The approach can also be more linear and directed than the cyclical reviews. But care must be taken. Although a crisis may exist, it is not always clear what the problem is. The first step

---

11 See for a good discussion of the process for operational reviews, Ontario Ministry of Tourism and Recreation, *Operational Reviews: Paths to Organizational Fitness* (Toronto: Queen's Printer, 1989).

is to identify a clear problem and what caused it. Options should be developed. The best option, based on pros and cons, would be selected and implemented. The final stage is to monitor and evaluate the results.

The process in all cases will go through a number of steps. First, it is important to gain support for the process. Not everybody will necessarily agree that a review is appropriate or needed. Sometimes even a crisis is difficult to see. Senior management and/or the board should normally be aware of the process if not approve of it. Second, appropriate resources should be allocated to ensure that the process has a chance at success. Those resources may be staff, volunteers, directors, stakeholders or consultants. There should be clear terms of reference that permit the review to remain focussed. The terms would normally include the gathering of information, determination of relevant facts, development of an action plan and the preparation of a report and recommendations. The appropriate person should make a decision — which may be senior management, an officer or the board. Finally, the selected option should be implemented and evaluated. Of course, implementation may include new or reallocated resources.

When is an operational review necessary? It probably should be built into the planning process. The organization may also want to examine itself periodically to ensure that it is making a difference. For example, it could ask itself a number of questions to see if it remains focussed and relevant:

- are the goals and objectives clear? Are they understood by those involved? Are there plans to achieve those goals and objectives? Do others in the community know and understand the goals and objectives?
- does the organization understand its environment? Does it know and understand the needs of its community? Does it consult with its stakeholders? Do others understand where the organization fits into the community? Is there a "target audience" and is it being reached?
- do the plans clearly identify objectives, activities, persons to carry out those activities? Are there specific dates for completion? For assessment and review? Does the organization have a good track record for implementation? Do others in the community recognize that track record? Are resourcing issues part of the plans and planning process? Does the organization cooperate with other organizations?
- are problems solved in a timely and appropriate manner? Are the best solutions found? Is there cooperation in finding solutions? Is there

open and frank discussion? Is there a culture of problem solving as opposed to blaming?

- do people feel important and useful and valued? Is there a trusting and respectful relationship among staff? Volunteers? Directors? With stakeholders?
- are activities and programs evaluated against stated objectives and goals on a regular basis? Is there monitoring on an ongoing basis? Are resources reviewed to ensure appropriate allocations? Does the community contribute to finding the best answers?

These questions are intended to encourage discussion, not to be the sole basis for determining what to assess or how to assess it. Those types of discussions should take place at the senior management level, by the board and at the staff and volunteer level. It is important to recognize that proper stewardship and accountability includes finding out what works and what does not work. It is the failure to do so that leads to poor governance and a lack of accountability. People understand that not all things work out according to plan; it is the failure to do something about it that is the real problem.

D FINANCIAL PLANNING TOOLS

I. Standards in Accounting

Financial accountability is one of the pillars of an organization's accountability to its members, regulators, funders and the public. Financial information is also essential to the proper governance of an organization. Although accountability involves more than financial accountability it is essential and financial accountability necessitates "books and records".

The Canadian Institute of Chartered Accountants is instrumental in setting the standards for financial accountability. The Accounting Standards Board and the Auditing Standards Board establish the standards in their respective areas and these standards are published in the CICA *Handbook*.[12] The *Handbook* includes both recommendations and background materials with respect to an accounting or auditing matter.

Charitable and not-for-profit organizations will be expected to maintain their financial records in a manner that is consistent with the

---

12 CICA *Handbook* (Toronto: Canadian Institute of Chartered Accountants, December 1999).

accounting standards. This expectation is particularly important if the organization is to be audited. If the organization does not follow the standards, it is not likely to obtain a "clean audit", which in turn will raise questions about the degree of accountability and integrity that does exist.

Many individuals involved in the charitable and not-for-profit sector are familiar with financial audits. Audits are usually undertaken by chartered accountants and in Ontario the *Public Accountancy Act*[13] effectively limits auditing to chartered accountants. The financial audit is intended to determine whether or not the financial statements fairly reflect the financial position and transactions of the organization. Financial statements are normally prepared on the basis of generally accepted accounting principles, or GAAP.[14] Audited financial statements would, therefore, normally be prepared on the basis of GAAP. GAAP involves the specific rules, practices and procedures relating to particular circumstances, including the recommendations set out in the *CICA Handbook*. Where there is no recommendation, other accounting principles apply that are generally accepted in Canada or that are consistent with the recommendations.[15]

There are, however, two other types of audits with which directors and senior management ought to be aware:

- compliance audits — this type of audit is intended to determine whether or not an organization has complied with a statute, regulation, contract or other similar document which sets out requirements. Compliance audits deal with more than financial matters and can delve into a very detailed analysis of an organization's decision-making process and delivery of programs.
- forensic audits — a forensic audit is used to determine what did happen and involves the tracking of funds and transactions from beginning to completion. It can include the review of every piece of paper related to the operations of the organization. A forensic audit is time-consuming and expensive and is something to be avoided. The easiest way to avoid a forensic audit is to comply with generally accepted accounting principles and with any legitimate requirements that may be imposed on an organization — and be able to demonstrate readily that one did so. Forensic audits would not be justified or needed if there were no problems or no indication of

---

13 R.S.O. 1990, c. P.37.

14 *CICA Handbook*, para. 1000.59.

15 *Ibid.*, para. 1000.60.

financial or similar problems. They are used where there has been a failure in the accountability structure or where it is missing in order to determine what happened.

II. Implementing the Standards — Some Challenges

The issue of financial accountability is obviously an important one. In many organizations, though, a board of directors will have a number of related issues that need to be considered.[16] There are challenges unique to charitable and not-for-profit organizations that arise out of the nature of the organizations and reliance on volunteers and limited access to resources. Most volunteers want to "do good"; they are seldom interested in and even less enthralled with paperwork, the basis for financial accountability. In addition, because they are there to "do good", some volunteers will feel insulted when the issue of financial accountability arises. A natural human reaction is "why don't you trust me", which is emphasized even more when the individual is doing the work as a volunteer rather than as an employee.

Volunteers need to comply with the requirements, but on the other hand are less inclined to do so and the organization has fewer levers to enforce compliance. With an employee, an organization's management or officers can enforce compliance through appropriate disciplinary action, if necessary. The ability to do so with volunteers is much more limited. If persuasion and education are not sufficient, the directors may have little choice but to remove the volunteer from the situation. But, removal of volunteers can be a difficult and delicate task.

The level of expertise and resources available to charitable and not-for-profit organizations is another limiting factor. Even the best intentioned volunteer or employee can only perform if he or she has adequate training and resources to carry out their functions. The treasurer of an organization is sometimes a director who may not have any accounting experience. It is also the type of position for which organizations do not have a large number of interested directors from which to draw. Next to the position of secretary, the position of treasurer is often as popular as being the last player selected for a pick-up hockey game.

Obviously, the above is not the situation in all organizations. But the issue of expertise and resources is a real one. The law and accounting

---

16 K.J. Caplan, *Accounting Guide for Not-for-Profit Organzations* (Toronto: Carswell, 1995), at sections 115.08 to 115.13.

principles and practices are often complicated and are not always easily understood. Turnover may exacerbate the situation; just as a treasurer becomes comfortable with the role, he or she moves on to another community or organization or has less time to devote to the activity. Professional assistance is available, but often organizations do not have the financial resources to pay for it. Staff in the sector tend to be lower paid and to carry out more functions than would occur in a business environment. The executive director is often the only staff person and must do it all, which necessarily limits the resources available for the "books and records". There are always higher priorities, such as delivering on the organization's charitable and not-for-profit purposes.

The directors, and senior management, need to ensure compliance with the appropriate accounting standards and with any organizational undertakings to government, funders, regulators or others. They should be aware that, owing to the unique tax status of charities, their financial affairs are apt to be subject to greater scrutiny and more constraints than some other organizations. The CCP's Ethical Fundraising and Financial Accountability Code is one response to recent calls for more transparency and accountability in the dealings of charities.

Although the Code and similar initiatives are focussed on charities — as distinct from not-for-profit organizations — the overall trend towards greater accountability and transparency is not likely to escape any member of the sector. The level of scrutiny of not-for-profits may not be as high, but it is there and will probably increase over the next several years. The same governance and accountability issues will play out in the not-for-profit part of the sector based on the underlying principles.

By establishing accounting policies and procedures that are both mindful of the organization's obligations and enhance its public credibility, directors can avoid the inconvenience and inefficiency of taking remedial steps to address these concerns after the fact. At the same time, directors must be cognizant of the restriction and limitations on the organization from a practical standpoint. Achieving the appropriate balance is not an easy task, but to do so, directors need to understand, at a minimum, the basic requirements for financial accountability.

III. Financial Records

a) Introduction

The maintenance of proper accounting records and the preparation of financial statements is the basis for financial accountability. The financial statements are the end result of the accounting records. They will assist a charitable or not-for-profit organization to demonstrate that it is meeting the requirements of the law, to develop plans for its operations, and to determine whether or not it is achieving its objects in an efficient manner.

There are several basic records and statements that charitable and not-for-profit organizations should maintain and prepare, irrespective of their legal form or their size. The level of sophistication of the records and statements will vary and reflect the needs of the organization. An organization with revenues of $20,000 per year is unlikely to need, or afford, a computerized record-keeping system. A large charity may, on the other hand, benefit from such a system.

The maintenance of proper accounting records is almost invariably a legal requirement. For example, the *Canada Corporations Act*[17] and the Ontario *Corporations Act*[18] both require corporations without share capital to keep accounting records. A failure to do so is a breach of those statutes and the directors may be held personally liable for any damages that occur as a result of the failure. Trustees of a trust are also required by common law to maintain accounting records. Similarly, the *Income Tax Act*[19] requires that books and records be maintained.

b) Types of Accounts and Journals

There are five classifications of accounts:[20]

- Assets — the economic resources owned or controlled by the organization, including cash, accounts receivable, inventory, furniture, equipment and so forth. Current assets are cash and other assets that can be readily converted into cash, such as accounts receivable. Long term assets are less readily converted into cash and include fixed assets;

---

17 Section 117, R.S.C. 1970, c. C-32.
18 Section 302, R.S.O. 1990, c. C.38.
19 R.S.C. 1985 (5th Supp.), c.1.
20 CICA *Handbook*, paras. 1000.25 to 1000.40.

- Liabilities — the debts of the organization, including accounts payable, mortgages and loans are liabilities. Current liabilities are liabilities that will be retired or paid off in the near future, for example, an invoice from a supplier. Long-term liabilities have a longer period before being paid off, such as a mortgage;
- Equity/Net Assets — the difference between assets and liabilities, which may be either a surplus (assets are greater than liabilities) or a deficit (liabilities are greater than assets). Unlike business entities, charitable organizations may not distribute equity to members. Most not-for-profit organizations will not distribute equity to its members, with the possible exception of a winding-up of the organization. Instead, any remaining equity or net assets would normally be distributed to another charity upon dissolution after payment of all debts and liabilities. Implicit in this category are gains and losses. A gain is an increase in the equity/net assets of the organization from transactions, including operations and contributions, and a loss is a decrease. Typically, where revenues exceed expenses, there will be a gain; if expenses exceed revenues, there will be a loss;
- Revenue — the money received or to be received by the organization, including membership fees, donations, grants and sales. Revenue is recorded in one of two ways — on a cash basis as it is received by the organization or on an accrual basis, as it is earned by the organization. Increasingly, the accrual rather than the cash basis is being used to comply with the generally accepted accounting principles;
- Expenses — the costs incurred to operate the organization and to carry out its objects. As with revenues, expenses may be recorded on a cash basis as the expense is paid or on an accrual basis as it is incurred.

The generally accepted accounting principles require that general purpose financial statements for charitable and not-for-profit organizations be prepared using the accrual basis.[21] The rationale for doing so is that it recognizes the effect of the transactions and events in the period in which the transactions and events occur. General purpose financial statements should be based, therefore, on accounting records that use the accrual basis. General purpose financial statements are

---

21 *Ibid.*, para. 1000.46.

financial statements that are intended to be used by external users and to meet their needs.

Special purpose financial statements could be prepared using either the cash or accrual basis. Additionally, if day-to-day accounting records are kept on a cash basis, they could be adjusted as at the reporting date to prepare the general purpose financial statements. It is sometimes easier for smaller organizations to keep the accounting records on a cash basis and to make the necessary adjustments in preparing the financial statements.

Some larger organizations will use a code system for each of the accounting classifications. Subcodes would be used to identify different types of expenses, such as administrative, office supplies, salaries and benefits. Care should be taken in the use of codes, especially with respect to what is considered "administrative", given restrictions on administrative expenses for charitable organizations. Coding is also usually necessary for computerized systems. In recent years, various software programs have been developed which are affordable even for smaller organizations. These programs can be used not only to record transactions but as a tool for directors and for senior management in preparing budgets, assessing in-year status and so forth. Whatever methods or systems are used, it is important to keep in mind that the purpose is to provide information that is useable in a manner that is cost effective.

Several books of account will be necessary and should be maintained by charitable and not-for-profit organizations. The following books are commonly used to record the transactions related to the five classifications of accounts:

- Cash Receipts/Disbursements Journal — to record all revenue received and all payouts made, usually by cheque. Some organizations will maintain separate journals where the number of transactions warrant;
- Payroll Journal — to record employee wages, payroll deductions (such as pensions, Canada Pension Plan premiums, employment insurance premiums and income tax), net pay and any other deductions. This journal is obviously not needed if the organization does not have employees;
- General Journal — all entries made to adjust necessary accounts, usually on a monthly basis, that are not recorded in other journals are made to the General Journal. An organization may also keep other

types of journals, such as a Petty Cash Journal, to record specific types of transactions;

- General Ledger — to record the changes to revenue, expenses, assets and liabilities and equity accounts. The General Ledger will be related to the subsidiary ledgers for specific matters, such as accounts payable, travel expenses or other subsidiary ledgers appropriate to the organization.

Organizations may also maintain other types of books of account and journals that are useful to it, its major funders and regulators or that are otherwise required by law. An organization may also maintain books of account for specific projects, programs or activities so that the revenues and expenses for a project, program or activity can be readily identified. Care should be taken when designing the books of account to ensure that the directors and senior management have the information that they need for accountability purposes and to manage the affairs of the organization, to assess progress in meeting the organization's goals and objectives and to plan. On the other hand, the amount of information or its presentation should not overwhelm and should be kept in context of the overall organization. Directors and senior management need to see and understand both the forest and the trees.

The financial records include the various supporting documents that are used to produce the account books. For example, an invoice or receipt should be available to support the expenditure of any funds. This type of document is also important for purposes of goods and services tax rebates that are available to registered charities and to some not-for-profit organizations. Each expenditure should be supported by a document to substantiate that the expenditure was made. In addition, receipts, deposit slips and similar documents should be available to substantiate the receipt of revenues.

IV. Financial Statements

a) Introduction

Financial statements may be for general purposes or for specific purposes depending upon the intended user. In either case, up-to-date bookkeeping and accounting records are necessary to prepare financial statements in order to ensure that the information provided to the user of the financial statements is accurate and complete and fairly represents the financial position of the organization and its financial transactions.

Financial statements are intended to provide information about: (i) the economic resources, obligations and equity/net assets of an organization, (ii) the changes in the organization's economic resources, obligations and equity/net assets, and (iii) the economic performance of the organization.[22]

b) Types of Financial Statements

The names given to the different types of financial statements will vary. However, in general, the following types of financial statements should be prepared — regardless of the name used to describe them:[23]

- statement of financial position. The purpose of this statement is to identify the economic resources that are available to the organization. It should include the following information:

    - net assets invested in capital assets;
    - net assets that are subject to restrictions requiring that they be maintained as endowment funds;
    - other restricted net assets;
    - unrestricted net assets, and
    - total net assets.[24]

    The nature of the restrictions should also be disclosed. An organization may impose restrictions on itself (internal restrictions) or the restrictions may be externally imposed. Internal restrictions are more readily removed by the organization, in most cases, than are external restrictions. An internal restriction could be, for example, a reserve fund that is established by the organization to cover 12 months operating expenses during a period of change. Once the rationale for the reserve fund is over or a more urgent use develops, the board could remove the internal restriction and reallocate the funds.

    Donors or funding agencies may also restrict the use of funds donated, say, for a building fund or for scholarships. The organization cannot on its own remove an external restriction and, as a result, those assets are not as flexible. They could not, for example, be used

---

22 *Ibid.*, para. 1000.15.

23 *Ibid.*, para. 4400.05.

24 *Ibid.*, paras. 4400.18 to 21.

for other programs delivered by the organization or for general operating expenses.

The existence of external restrictions is not necessarily a negative. Most donors want to ensure that their gift is used appropriately and will have a positive impact in the areas that are of concern to them. The fact that the organization has in place the accounting systems to identify, monitor and comply with external restrictions — and audited financial statements to verify that it does — is itself a potential selling point for donors.

The issue of restricted assets is discussed below as part of "restricted fund accounting" and "deferred contributions". Any restrictions on an asset's use must be disclosed. The CICA *Handbook* provides two approaches for charitable and not-for-profit organizations to use to disclose this information — restricted fund method or deferral method.[25]

- statement of operations. This statement presents information about the changes in the organization's resources and obligations over the period, such as a fiscal year. It includes information about the revenues and expenses of the organization's operations. It will also disclose the source of revenues, for example, from operations or from contributions such as donations. Expenses may be described by object, function or program. Expenses should be classified in a manner that provides the most meaningful information for the users — including for the organization's own use. The information should also be recorded and used in a manner that is efficient for other purposes.[26]

  A registered charity will need to complete the annual Charity Information Return and will usually want to minimize the need to make changes to its accounting information to comply with the requirements of the Canada Customs and Revenue Agency. The information is important both for purposes of presenting information about the organization but also for budget and planning purposes.

---

[25] *Ibid.*, para. 4400.02.

[26] *Ibid.*, paras. 4400.30 and 31.

Revenues and expenses should be reported as gross amounts.[27] The use of "net amounts" does not provide a clear picture of the transactions and financial position of the organization. For example, if the organization only reports on the net amount earned or lost from a fundraising event or from a program that incurs costs and receives revenues, it does not provide the user of the financial statements with an understanding of the exposure that the organization had, its true costs or similar information. It also does not assist in determining the efficiency and effectiveness of the project, program or activity — something that all boards of directors should know.

The disclosure could occur as a note to the financial statements. In this way, the net amount could be reported as part of the statement but a note would set out details about the revenues and expenses. While there may be circumstances in which the reporting of gross amounts would distort the true picture of the organization and its financial position, the decision not to report the gross amount should be taken with specific accounting advice.

If the organization uses the deferral method to account for restrictions on funds, the statement of operations should present the following information:

- for each financial statement item, a total that includes all funds reported; and
- total excess or deficiency of revenues and gains over expenses and losses for the period.[28]

If the organization uses the restricted fund method, the following information would be presented in the statement of operations:

- the total for each financial statement item recognized in the general fund;
- the total for each financial statement item recognized in the restricted funds, other than the endowment fund;
- the total for each financial statement item recognized in the endowment fund;

---

27 *Ibid.*, paras. 4400.37 to 40.

28 *Ibid.*, para. 4400.33.

- excess or deficiency of revenues and gains over expenses and losses for each of the general fund, restricted funds other than the endowment fund and the endowment fund.[29]

- statement of change in net assets. This statement is sometimes called the statement of changes in fund balances. It is often combined with the statement of operations. Whether separate or integrated into the statement of operations, the information that is typically presented includes:

  - net assets invested in capital assets;
  - net assets subject to restrictions requiring that they be maintained permanently as endowments;
  - other restricted net assets;
  - unrestricted net assets; and
  - total net assets.[30]

  If the organization uses fund accounting, it should provide a description of the purpose of each fund.[31] This information apprises the user about important information on any restrictions that apply to the fund and the types of expenses that are reported in the fund. If there are any interfund transfers, those should be presented in the statement of changes in net assets. The amount and purpose of the interfund transfer should also be disclosed. If any interfund loans are made or remain outstanding, these too should be disclosed, including the amounts, terms and conditions.[32] A fund could include, for example, a reserve fund which is not restricted by external sources but which the board has established out of prudence.

- statement of cash flows. This statement reports on the total changes in cash and cash equivalents from the organization's activities and is intended to provide information about the source and uses of cash by the organization. It is also called a statement of changes in financial position. The purpose of this statement is to provide information about the source of cash and its uses. It allows users to assess the organization's ability to generate cash, either from internal (from

---

29 *Ibid.*, para. 4400.35.
30 *Ibid.*, para. 4400.41.
31 *Ibid.*, para. 4400.06.
32 *Ibid.*, paras 4400.12 to 15.

operations) or external sources. It can also be used to assess management's abilities to manage the organization in a fiscally prudent manner. Donors and granting agencies will also use the statement of cash flow to determine if the organization used the funds that it received from them for the purpose that it was given and intended to be used.

The statement of cash flows will distinguish at the least the following:

- cash from operations; and
- the components of cash flow that came from financing and investing activities.[33]

The financial statements will normally include "Notes to the Financial Statements". These Notes provide information on issues necessary for the reader to understand fully the information contained in the financial statements.[34] Notes will typically include a statement of the organization's major accounting practices, the legal structure of the organization and whether it is a registered charity, and any contingencies, such as outstanding litigation. Several accounting practices should be disclosed, including how the organization treats donated property, plants and equipment, materials and services; how pledges are accounted for; how fixed assets are accounted for; what restricted resources are included in the financial statements and an indication of the nature of the restriction; and the income tax status of the organization. The notes to the financial statement are an integral part of the financial statements.

The financial statements may include supporting schedules, such as a more detailed schedule of expenses for important projects. Often, a more detailed schedule is included for fundraising activities, which will assist in determining the efficiency and effectiveness of different types of fundraising activities. The schedules are intended to provide supplementary information that is not necessarily required to comply with generally accepted accounting principles but that is nonetheless informative for users of financial statements.

If the financial statements are audited, the "Auditor's Report", prepared by an independent auditor, will present an opinion on the accuracy of the financial statements. The auditor may express an unqualified opinion ("clean audit"), a qualified opinion or deny providing

---

33 *Ibid.*, paras. 4400.44 to 46.

34 *Ibid.*, paras. 1500.04.

an opinion, depending upon the auditor's professional assessment. In carrying out the assessment and issuing an opinion, the auditor must comply with the standards established by the Auditing Standards Board and the generally accepted auditing standards.

The auditor may make such enquiries as is necessary to enable him or her to report on whether the financial statements fairly present the financial position of the organization and the results of its operations for the period under review in accordance with generally accepted accounting principles applied on a basis consistent with that of the preceding period. In some cases, where changes have occurred, the auditor will note that changes were made and the financial statements will represent the financial information from the previous period on a consistent basis.

Financial statements and the presentation of financial information must meet a number of qualitative characteristics to comply with the requirements set out in the CICA *Handbook*. They must be understandable by the usual external users; relevant in that they have predictive value and feedback value and are timely; reliable in that they present the transactions and events faithfully, verifiably, neutrally and conservatively; and comparable so that like information can be compared. The *Handbook* does recognize that trade-offs among these qualitative characteristics may be necessary. But these trade-offs are themselves the subject of professional assessment and judgement.[35]

c) Contributions — Restricted Fund Accounting Method and the Deferral Method

The CICA *Handbook* addresses in a separate section what is a contribution and different types of contributions that may be made to organizations. The *Handbook* requires that contributions be recognized either in accordance with the deferral method or the restricted fund method.[36]

A contribution is defined in the *Handbook* as:

> ... a non-reciprocal transfer to a not-for-profit organization of cash or other assets or a non-reciprocal settlement or cancellation of its liabilities. Government funding provided to a not-for-profit organization is considered to be a contribution.[37]

---

[35] *Ibid.*, paras. 1000.17 to 1000.24 review these issues in detail.

[36] *Ibid.*, para. 4410.10.

[37] *Ibid.*, para. 4410.02(b).

This definition is, not surprisingly, generally consistent with the approach taken in the *Income Tax Act* and by the Canada Customs and Revenue Agency for a donation to be eligible for the issuance of a receipt for income tax purposes. There are some nuances, however, that are not entirely consistent but which are probably not decisive. For example, the Canada Customs and Revenue Agency would distinguish between a gift and a sponsorship where the business is allowed to provide some materials about itself. It is receiving something in return for the sponsorship. The business could, in that circumstance, treat the "contribution" as a business expense. It is not as certain that it is, for accounting purposes, a "reciprocal contribution". In some cases, a charity may consider the sponsorship in that circumstance to be a non-reciprocal contribution from the perspective of the charity.

Three types of contributions are identified in the *Handbook*:[38]

- a restricted contribution, where there are external restrictions on the uses of the asset. For example, the donation of cash may be for a building fund and for no other purpose. There are some examples where the restriction may be to prohibit certain uses. Charitable gaming is one example where the terms and conditions of a lottery licence may limit the use of funds to certain approved uses;
- an endowment contribution, which is a specific type of restricted contribution. An endowment contribution is to be part of a permanent fund and the organization is to use the revenue from that fund. The specific assets in the endowment fund may change as investment climates and opportunities change, unless, of course, a particular donation provides otherwise;
- unrestricted contribution, which can be used for any purpose or activities within the objects of the organization.

The recognition of a restricted contribution may be deferred in the financial statements until the organization incurs the relevant expense. This deferral makes sense from a conceptual perspective. If the contribution has restrictions such that the organization cannot use the donation until it is ready to construct a building or purchase equipment, then it is not, in one sense, an "asset" of the organization until it incurs the expense. Once it incurs that expense, it can gain access to the restricted contribution. As a result, if this approach is taken, the

[38] *Ibid.*

restricted contributions could be accumulated as deferred contributions and not increase the net assets of the organization.[39] The financial statements would include a note or schedule on the accumulated deferred contributions.

Alternatively, the organization could report restricted contributions on the restricted fund accounting basis. Contributions would be recorded and increase the net assets of the restricted fund. Once the building is constructed or the equipment purchased, the payment for that transaction would be recorded against the restricted fund account.[40]

Endowment funds are a special form of restricted fund. These contributions are permanently maintained on a separate basis. The contributions themselves are not intended to be available to be used for the organization's operations. Instead, the income from the endowment fund is intended to be used to pay for the operations, or, in some cases, for specific programs. An endowment fund could, therefore, be an "unrestricted" one or a "restricted" one. In either case, the endowment fund is reported on as a separate fund and the assets are accumulated separately from the other resources of the organization.[41]

It is critical that the board of directors and senior management of the organization be aware of and comply with the various restrictions that may exist on funds. There may be legal obligations to do so, in addition to the general fiduciary duties of directors. A failure to do so may expose both the organizations and equally important the directors and officers to legal difficulties. The organization itself may be irreparably harmed if the directors allow a reputation to be established that the organization does not comply with restrictions. Aside from the potential breach of trust implications, such a reputation could seriously undermine the organization's credibility and its future ability to obtain support — financial or otherwise — in the future.

The board also needs to be aware of the restrictions for planning purposes. How could a board of directors develop its strategic direction, and long and short term plans if it does not know what restrictions may exist on the funds? Could it prepare a budget or plan cash flow if it does not know that certain funds are restricted? Or that certain events must occur for the restriction to be lifted? Obviously, it would be extremely difficult if not impossible for the board to do so and directors are probably

39 *Ibid.*, para. 4410.28.

40 *Ibid.*, para. 4410.57.

41 *Ibid.*, para. 4410.05(e)(ii), and paras. 4410.29 to 30 for the deferral method, and paras. 4410.60 to 61 for the restricted fund method.

not fulfilling their fiduciary duties if they are not aware of such restrictions or do not operate within them.

The board also needs to know and understand the potential impact that a restriction may have on its operations or strategic direction. There are some circumstances in which a board may decide not to accept a donation because the restrictions are impractical or, in a worst-case situation, illegal or unethical. A board in Ontario in the twenty-first century would be very hard-pressed to accept a donation for a scholarship fund if it could use the revenue solely for scholarships for Caucasian, Protestant males.[42] Some boards will put in place policies or make decisions on a case-by-case basis with respect to the source of contributions. For example, some health charities will not accept contributions or participate in sponsorships from businesses that create, in the charity's opinion, health risks.

There are special considerations around grants or other funding from governments. The government grant may be based upon the budget provided by the organization and the organization is required to report on its expenditures on an ongoing basis.[43] Often, the organization may not spend the grant unless it obtains matching funding or only if it makes a specific, agreed upon purchase. Any unused grant sometimes must be returned to the government agency. Government grants may also be received prior to the intention to spend the money or the start of the organization's fiscal year. In this case, the organization may decide to treat the grant as a restricted fund until the fiscal period in which the monies are to be spent.

Accounting, to some extent, is an exercise of determining when to "recognize" revenues and expenses. The generally accepted accounting principles provide guidance on making the proper determination. The need to do so is to ensure that the financial information provided to users accurately and fairly represents the financial position and the transactions of the organization. As noted above, an organization may recognize restricted contributions either on a restricted fund or deferral basis.

If the organization does not report on a restricted fund accounting basis, then restricted contributions would be recognized in the fiscal period in which the related expenses are incurred. If the restricted

---

42 See *Canada Trust Co. v. Ontario (Human Rights Commission)* (1990), 74 O.R. (2d) 481 (*sub nom. Leonard Foundation Trust, Re*), 12 C.H.R.R. D/184, 69 D.L.R. (4th) 321, 38 E.T.R. 1, 37 O.A.C. 191 (C.A.).

43 CICA *Handbook*, paras. 4410.08 to 09.

contribution was for expenses to be incurred in a future fiscal period, it would not be recognized as revenue until that future fiscal period. It would be a deferred contribution. The funds would, therefore, be segregated from the organization's current fiscal period's statement of revenues and expenses. It would be recorded as a deferred contribution, which in turn may be accumulated over a number of fiscal periods. The deferred contribution would then be recognized or included in the fiscal period when the event that triggers the removal of the restriction occurs.

If the restricted contribution is for the purchase of capital assets, the capital asset may be amortized over more than one or two fiscal periods. If so, the contribution should be deferred and recognized on the same basis as the amortized expense. Amortization is used to reflect the cost of a capital asset over that asset's useful life.[44] The organization will benefit from the capital asset not only in the fiscal period in which it was purchased, but over a longer period of time, such as five or ten years. Of course, if the capital asset is not amortized, it will be recognized when the capital purchase is made.[45]

The alternative to recognizing restricted contributions in the manner discussed above is for the organization to use restricted fund accounting.[46] The organization's financial statements would include an unrestricted fund for its operational expenses and one or more restricted funds. The restricted fund records the receipt and use of funds that are subject to restrictions. As noted above, an endowment fund is a special type of restricted fund because its purpose is to be a permanently restricted fund to generate income for use by the organization. With restricted fund accounting, a restricted contribution is recognized in the fiscal period in which the contribution is made, but in the restricted fund. The contribution is, therefore, revenue for the restricted fund and would increase the net assets of that restricted fund. Any expenditures that are made from that restricted fund would need to comply with the restrictions. For example, a contribution for the building fund would be recognized in the fiscal period in which it was made by the donor and increase the net assets. If the building is constructed that same period, the expenses would be recognized and reduce the net assets. If the building were constructed two years later, the expenses would be recognized in that latter fiscal period.

---

44 *Ibid.*, paras. 4410.33 to 37.

45 The accounting for capital assets is the subject of separate sections in the CICA *Handbook*. Section 4430 deals with most capital assets and section 4440 with collections.

46 *Ibid.*, paras. 4410.57 to 77.

Pledges and bequests are common forms of contributions and fundraising campaigns are sometimes developed around them. Pledges and bequests are "contribution receivables" and should be recognized in the financial statements when:[47]

- the amount to be received can be reasonably estimated; and
- ultimate collection is reasonably assured.

To some extent, these two criteria involve both accounting and legal advice. If the organization is advised that it was left a bequest, it may not be in a position to recognize that bequest at that time. It may be necessary for the estate to go through probate. Others may object to the bequest or contest the amount. There may be insufficient funds in the estate to pay the bequest. Until the cash is in hand or there is sufficient evidence, including a legal opinion, that the amount will be collected, a conservative approach would be not to recognize the bequest in that fiscal period.

Similarly, a pledge should not be included in the fiscal year in which it is made unless there are reasonably strong assurances that the property will be transferred. Campaigns, especially capital campaigns, often involve pledges over a period of years. The law around pledges is not entirely clear, but it would be very difficult to enforce a pledge as there usually is no contract between the donor and the organization. For a contract to exist, there must be mutual consideration and consideration, if of a significant value, could mean that the contribution is not "non-reciprocal".

In any event, downturns in the economy, personal problems and so forth will affect the ability and willingness of the individual or business to fulfil its pledge. The donor may also be disturbed by how its previous donations were used and decline to fulfil the pledge. There are many reasons why a donor will not fulfil a pledge and these reasons will normally increase over time. The longer the period of the pledge, the greater the risk that it will not be met. Unless the organization can be reasonably assured that the payment will be made, based on an assessment of the circumstances and relevant previous experiences, the pledge should not be recognized for purposes of the financial statements.

Government funding, on the other hand, is more readily fulfilled.[48] Although there are circumstances in which a government will not

---

47 *Ibid.*, para. 4420.03.

48 *Ibid.*, para. 4410.08.

provide the grant that it committed to provide, those usually are based on the actions or failure to act by the organization. For example, if the organization did not incur the expenses for which the grant was intended or the organization did not obtain the required matching funds from other sources, the government grant may be withheld.

The contribution is not always "cash". Often, a donor will give materials or services to the organization. The organization should only recognize such donations in its financial statements if a fair market value can be determined for the donation.[49] Furthermore, if the donor is donating services, it is important to remember that a receipt for income tax purposes cannot be provided for the contribution of services — although, if the organization pays for the services, the service provider could in turn donate the equivalent amount to the charity and the charity could issue a receipt for income tax purposes.[50]

The date of determining the fair market value may be different between an accounting and tax perspective, although only in some situations. The fair market value of a gift of equipment, for example, is to be determined as of the date the charity receives it for purposes of the *Income Tax Act*. For accounting purposes, the date is the date on which fair value can be reasonably determined if fair value can be reasonably estimated.[51] In most cases, the difference is not relevant, but if the property were securities in a volatile period on the stock market, there could be a relevant difference for which specific legal and accounting advice is required.

d) Reporting on Controlled and Related Entities

Organizations will sometimes control or be related to other entities. The CICA *Handbook* addresses these situations in a separate section for accounting purposes.[52] Of course, if the organization is a registered charity, it will need to address the issue of "associated charity" for purposes of the *Income Tax Act*.

Control is defined as the "continuing power to determine ... strategic operating, investing and financing policies without the co-operation of others".[53] This definition is broad and is not limited to "legal control".

---

49 *Ibid.*, paras. 4410.16 to 18.

50 Para. 30, *Registered Charities: Operating a Registered Charity*, Information Circular 80-10R, December 17, 1985.

51 CICA *Handbook*, para. 4410.19.

52 *Ibid.*, section 4450.

53 *Ibid.*, para. 4450.02.

Obviously, the levers of control will also be different from those normally encountered in a business context where a "parent" will "control" its "subsidiaries" through ownership of shares. However, if the reporting organization has the authority to appoint a majority of the directors of the board of the other organization, it will be presumed to exercise control.

The *Handbook* also discusses "economic interests" as opposed to ownership. An economic interest exists if one organization holds resources that must be used to produce revenue or provide services for the other or the reporting organization is responsible for the liabilities of the other organization.[54] This situation could occur, for example, in the endowment foundation scenario where a foundation is established to be used to raise an endowment fund. The revenue from the endowment fund is donated to the associated charity. It is increasingly common to use this approach for fundraising purposes, especially if there is a risk to the endowment fund for purposes of liability or for other reasons.

If the reporting organization controls another organization, it should report on the controlled organization in one of the following methods:[55]

- consolidating the controlled organization in the reporting organization's financial statements;
- providing disclosure as provided for in Section 4450.22;
- providing disclosure as provided for in Section 4450.26 where the organization is one of several organizations that are immaterial. In this situation, each of the individual organizations are insignificant or immaterial. A judgement call must be made whether or not the expense and effort of adapting financial information from these individual organizations that are insignificant or immaterial or incorporating into consolidated financial statements will result in materially relevant information for the users of the organization's financial statements. If the organization does not exercise any control over these other organizations, it is questionable that any additional expense or effort would be justified.

The following information should be disclosed, regardless of which approach is taken:[56]

---

54 *Ibid.*

55 *Ibid.*, para. 4450.14.

56 *Ibid.*, para. 4450.15.

- the policy followed in reporting the controlled organization;
- a description of the relationship with the controlled organization;
- a clear and concise description of the controlled organization's purpose, its intended community of service, its status under income tax legislation and its legal form; and
- the nature and extent of any economic interest that the reporting organization has in the controlled organization.

If the reporting organization has significant influence over another organization, it should disclose the following information in its financial statements:[57]

- a description of the relationship with the significantly influenced organization;
- a clear and concise description of the influenced organization's purpose, its intended community of service, its status under income tax legislation and its legal form; and
- the nature and extent of any economic interest that the reporting organization has in the significantly influenced organization.

In some cases, the organization may also have a significant influence over for-profit entities. Indeed, operating or being part of a business is a major method of raising funds for some organizations. If an organization has significant influence over a profit-oriented enterprise, it must disclose that investment in accordance with the long term investments rules in the *Handbook*.[58] Similarly, if it has an economic interest in a not-for-profit organization that does not amount to control or significant influence, it must disclose the nature and extent of the interest.[59] In both cases, the intention is to provide the user with relevant information about the relationships that the organization has, the resources and obligations that may exist and the risks that may flow from such relationships.

Organizations will often have an interest in controlled profit-oriented enterprises. An organization should report each controlled profit-oriented enterprise in one of two ways:[60]

---

57 *Ibid.*, para. 4450.40.
58 *Ibid.*, paras. 4450.43 to 44.
59 *Ibid.*, para. 4450.45.
60 *Ibid.*, paras. 4450.30 to 35.

- by consolidating the controlled enterprise in its financial statements; or
- by accounting for its investment in the controlled enterprise using the equity method. In this situation, the organization would report for each controlled enterprise or group of similar controlled enterprises by disclosing the total assets, liabilities and shareholders' equity at the reporting date, and revenues (including gains), expenses (including losses), net income and cash flows from operating, financing and investing activities reported in this period. The recommendations with respect to presentation and disclosure of long term investments in Section 3050 and for consolidated financial statements in Section 1600 would apply.

The directors must, in Ontario in particular, keep in mind that any investments of this nature must comply with the requirements of the *Trustee Act*[61] with respect to investments and with the restrictions on ownership of shares under the *Charitable Gifts Act*.[62] This issue is discussed in Chapter 3 with respect to investment policies for charitable organizations.

The organization may also be involved in joint ventures — either for profit purposes or as part of the delivery of the organization's objects. The organization should report on these joint ventures by accounting for its interest. The organization may use the proportionate consolidated method or the equity method.[63] In either case, the policy followed in reporting the interest and a description of the organization's relationship with the joint venture should be disclosed. The information to be disclosed is, not surprisingly, similar to that for profit-oriented enterprises.[64]

These types of investments can be complicated and the resulting obligations to report accurately the organization's interest and the financial implications of that interest may be correspondingly complicated. The purpose here is not to set out in detail how the organization's accountants ought to do so; rather, to apprise the directors of the need to do so. Also, this type of information is important for directors and senior managers to assess the risks that exist for the organization and the potential need to minimize those risks. In some cases, those risks may include personal liability if, for example, the investment was outside the legal authority of the organization to make the investment. This issue is particularly (but not

61 R.S.O. 1990, c. T.23.
62 R.S.O. 1990, c. C.8.
63 CICA *Handbook*, para. 4450.36.
64 *Ibid.*, paras. 4450.37 and 38.

solely) important for charitable organizations, which have both statutory and common law restrictions with respect to "carrying on business".

Organizations in the charitable and not-for-profit sector are often involved in a number of related party transactions. A related party relationship will exist when one party has the ability to exercise control, joint control or significant influence over another party — which may be done directly or indirectly by the organization. A related party relationship could be created through one having an economic interest in the other or through common or joint management. If the organization has related party transactions with another organization, i.e., the transfer of economic resources or obligations, it is important for those transactions to be disclosed in the financial statements.[65]

There is a judgement call that must be made on whether or not the parties are related. Several factors may be used to make this determination. If they are, and a related party transaction occurs, the organization should describe the relationship and the transaction (whether or not consideration was exchanged), the recorded amount of the transaction classified by financial statement category, the measurement basis used for recognizing the transaction in the financial statements, the amounts due to or from the related parties and the terms and conditions, contractual obligations with related parties and any contingencies amount related parties.[66] This type of information is needed so that the user of the financial statements can determine, among other things, whether or not the transactions were for fair market value. It may also provide information about the relative levels of exposure to risks and any changes to risk levels from one year to another.

e) Other **CICA Handbook** *Requirements*

The discussion thus far has focussed on the areas of financial accountability that are unique to charitable and not-for-profit organizations and the presentation of the information in financial statements. There are a number of other sections of the CICA *Handbook* that are not specific to the sector but that are applicable. Several provisions in the *Handbook* apply to all entities — regardless of their legal character or nature of the entity — because they are necessary to ensure that financial information is presented fairly, accurately and in a consistent manner. These provisions

---

65 *Ibid.*, para. 4460.03.

66 *Ibid.*, para. 4460.07.

include, for example, the basic financial statement concepts discussed earlier in this chapter.

The *Handbook* itself identifies the following sections as being generally applicable:

- Financial Statement Concepts – Section 1000;
- General Standards of Financial Statement Presentation – Section 1500;
- Disclosure of Accounting Policies – Section 1505;
- Accounting Changes – Section 1506;
- Measurement Uncertainty – Section 1508;
- Current Assets and Current Liabilities – Section 1510;
- Contractual Obligations – Section 3280;
- Contingencies – Section 3290;
- Subsequent Events – Section 3820.

There are several sections that apply to organizations in the sector if they have relevant transactions. These sections include the following:

- Consolidated Financial Statements – Section 1600;
- Foreign Currency Transactions – Section 1650;
- Cash – Section 3000;
- Temporary Investments – Section 3010;
- Accounts and Notes Receivable – Section 3020;
- Impaired Loans – Section 3025;
- Inventories – Section 3030;
- Prepaid Expenses – Section 3040;
- Long-Term Investments – Section 3050;
- Leases – Section 3065;
- Deferred Charges – Section 3070;
- Long-Term Debt – Section 3210;
- Revenue – Section 3400;
- Research and Development Costs – Section 3450;
- Employee Future Benefits – Section 3461;
- Discontinued Operations – Section 3475;
- Extraordinary Items – Section 3480;
- Non-Monetary Transactions – Section 3830;
- Interest Capitalized – Disclosure Considerations – Section 3850;
- Financial Instruments – Disclosure and Presentation – Section 3860
- Future-Oriented Financial Information – Section 4250.

A detailed review of these types of provisions is beyond the scope of this chapter and text. However, another text in this series will provide a more detailed analysis of financial accounting and the requirements on organizations in the sector. In addition, some of these provisions have been referred to or discussed in this chapter or reviewed in Chapter 3 with respect to risk.

Financial accountability is at the crux of accountability and govern-ance in any organization — for-profit, not-for-profit or charitable. As the users of financial information and the community become more aware and demanding, the level, accuracy and fairness of the financial information will increase. New standards for information will inevitably develop. Furthermore, as organizations become more global in nature — or participate in joint ventures or other projects with similar organizations elsewhere — the depth and sophistication will also increase. Organizations may need to comply not only with Canadian GAAP but GAAP in other jurisdictions, such as the United States and Europe. There has been some movement towards international standards for GAAP in the for-profit sector and it can be expected that this movement will also occur in the charitable and not-for-profit sector.

Whatever the specific standards or requirements that may be in place, the end product will remain the same:

- to provide financial and related information that accurately and fairly presents the financial position and transactions of the organization; and
- to provide useful and timely financial and related information for planning and assessment purposes.

This information is fundamental to the proper stewardship of an organization and to demonstrating good governance and accountability.

Chapter 3

MANAGING RISK

A INTRODUCTION

Risk exists. There is no activity or program that a charity or not-for-profit organization engages in that does not involve risk. The risks may arise out of the legal relationships or legal responsibilities of the organization with or towards others, from the financial resources or capital assets that are being put to use, or out of the methods used to carry out the activities. The level of risk may be high or low. The activities may have implicit risks or the risks may have been caused or increased due to the quality of implementation. The board of directors may have expressly reviewed the risks or may not even be aware of them. In some cases, the risk and level of risk may not become apparent for years or even decades after the event or activity.

The issue is not whether or not risk exists; rather it is how the board of directors, the officers and others manage those risks. The first step in managing risk is recognizing that it exists and defining the circumstances under which it can arise. The board should also have an understanding of the likelihood of the risk coming to be. A key factor in determining whether there is liability for damages stemming from a particular situation is forseeability. Where harm arising from a practice or activity can easily be anticipated, there is a greater expectation that steps will be taken to reduce the chance that such harm will occur. So, directors need to become skilled in assessing the relative risks of different situations. In some cases this assessment will be straightforward.

Risk is a contextual matter; the level of risk may increase or decrease depending upon the context. For example, clearly risk is higher if alcohol is served during physical activity, such as sports. The risk of physical injury to a child from playing hockey is obviously greater than that of an adult playing chess. However, in some cases directors will have to make more nuanced assessments. For example, how vulnerable a particular organization's clientele are or how financially risky a particular investment strategy is should be determined in advance and be part of the decision-making process.

B SOURCES OF RISK AND LIABILITY

I. Collective Decision Making and Liability

There are a number of sources of risk and, ultimately, the potential for liability for the organization, the members of the board of directors and the organization's officers. Liability is a legal concept that deserves some discussion in order to understand the interplay between risk and liability.

An organization — be it a corporation, trust or unincorporated association — is an artificial entity. It exists because it is a convenient way for humans to carry out activities for a common purpose as a group. But any organization may only act if a human being acts on its behalf. Decisions on when to act, what to do and how to do it are made by humans. The directors, in most cases, are responsible for the management of the affairs of the organization and are, therefore, essential in the decision making process that leads to action or inaction.

Boards generally make decisions as a collective. Somebody moves a resolution, there is discussion on the resolution and a vote is taken or consensus develops and it is minuted. While not all decisions are made in this linear process, most decisions are made in a process that includes these steps. There may be strong opinions on all sides of the issue, but a decision is made to act or not to act and that decision is recorded.

This collective approach to decision making is inherent in how organizations are managed and operate. The decision may delegate the actual carrying out of the actions to officers, staff, volunteers or agents of the organization, but the board is responsible and accountable for the decision. As such, liability may arise from the board's actions or failures to act and this liability may fall jointly and severally on the directors.

Joint and several liability is a legal concept that is intended, in part, to allocate responsibility for liability. If somebody is jointly and severally liable for damages, he or she is responsible for the full amount of the damages together with the other directors and individually as a director. Joint and several liability means that the injured person can collect the full amount of the damages from one director or from any or all of the directors.

However, if the action or failure to act is attributable to one director alone and the other directors did not have knowledge of it then the claim would be against only that director. This situation could arise, for example, if a director had a conflict of interest but participated in the decision making process.

If a director feels that a decision is wrong or will result in a breach of the law or of a duty, he or she ought to oppose the decision during the board meeting. When the vote is taken on the resolution, he or she should vote accordingly and ensure that such vote is recorded so that there is a minute of the position taken by the director. If the director did not attend the meeting at which the decision was taken, he or she should note the dissent at the next meeting and have the minutes record that dissent.

II. Ex Officio and Honorary Directors

There are two types of directors that are often used by organizations which deserve special attention — *ex officio* and honorary. It is not uncommon for organizations to have either or both types of directors, but do not always understand what those directors are intended to do and, as a result, their role and potential liability may be unclear.

An *ex officio* director is one who is a director by right of another office that he or she holds. A municipal councillor may, for example, be a director of a humane society or another organization that provides services in the municipality. Or the chair of a hospital board of directors may be an *ex officio* director of the foundation that has been established to raise funds for medical equipment. As an *ex officio* director, the individual will continue to have all the rights and obligations of any other director. There may be complications in meeting their obligations to the other organization and, at the same time, acting in the best interests of the organization of which they are an *ex officio* director. The law is far from clear and in some circumstances, the *ex officio* director may be faced with two conflicting positions — acting in the best interests of both organizations may not be possible. Even worse, if the *ex officio* director has confidential information from his or her position in one organization, can he or she bring that information to the table of the other organization? How will he or she vote at the other organization? Is it best to declare a conflict of interest and recuse oneself? Or should the matter be discussed at both organizations?

Clearly, the context will be an important factor in making any decision on how to proceed.

But these problems do not arise on a daily basis. There is much merit in having *ex officio* directors, who are a link between two organizations with a common interest or issue. *Ex officio* directors can share nonconfidential information, bring a different perspective and enhance the decision making through their participation on boards.

There is another issue with respect to *ex officio* directors — are they voting or non-voting?

An *ex officio* director would normally be a voting director unless the terms of the by-laws provide otherwise. There may be reasons for the *ex officio* director to be non-voting, but this decision should be a conscious one. Legally, as a director, he or she will have all the rights and obligations of any other director, which includes the right and obligation to vote on matters that come before the board in managing the affairs of the organization unless these rights and obligations have been removed in a lawful manner. The letters patent or by-laws, for example, that establish the positions of *ex officio* director may limit the rights and obligations as a director.

Although it is not uncommon to make the president, chief executive officer, or other senior staff person in an organization an *ex officio* director significant problems can arise from this practice. Arguably in this circumstance, the staff member becomes a paid director. A not-for-profit organization having a paid director may breach non-distribution provisions (*i.e.*, clauses intended to preclude distribution of the organization's assets to certain parties) of the legislation under which it is incorporated or of the entity's constating documents. An additional restriction is placed on charities in this regard. Trustees of a charity have a duty to act gratuitously. Paying a director of a charity for what is, at least in part, exercising his or her responsibilities as a trustee, could be held to breach this obligation. Accordingly, having staff hold *ex officio* positions should generally be discouraged.

Honorary directors are also common for fundraising purposes and to recognize the contributions an individual has made to the organization or to society. Care must be taken, though, to define what their rights and obligations are and to ensure that third parties are not misled as to those rights and obligations. For example, if an honorary director is used for fundraising purposes, the reason to do so is to enhance the "pitch" to the potential donor. The hope is that the potential donor will be more willing to donate to an organization with which the honorary director is associated. If the donor is displeased with the results of the donation, or felt that he or she was misled by the information provided in the donation package, would he or she have any recourse to the honorary director?

Possibly not, except in unusual circumstances. Those circumstances could include situations in which the potential donor was led to believe by the honorary director that he or she had a greater role than just being a name on the letterhead. Occasionally, the honorary director may also believe that the role has more substance and may purport to act on behalf of the organization.

It is important to make sure that the role is clear, whether the honorary directorship is for fundraising purposes, to honour the individual or for other purposes. The rights and obligations of the honorary director should be set out and communicated so that there are no misunderstandings and the chances of others being misled are minimized. If the honorary director is to have a right to vote or other rights and obligations of a director, that should be clear — and needs to be clear in the constating documents or the by-laws of the organization. But once an organization starts down the path of honorary directors, the risk begins. There is an argument that "a director is a director" and a court could find that a duty of care and liability exist.

Regardless of the voting rights, honorary directors need to be dealt with fairly by the organization. Whether the honorary director is there due to his or her fundraising potential or to recognize a contribution, his or her name is being used to benefit the organization. The honorary director should have access to a reasonable amount of information about the organization so that he or she can make a decision on whether or not to become or remain an honorary director. If an organization is going to trade on somebody's reputation, it needs to treat that person well and in a fair manner.

III. Statutory and Common Law Sources of Liability

There are a number of common sources for directors' liability. The following chart sets out the more common areas that may give rise to directors' liability.[1] When reviewing these common sources, however, it is important to keep in mind the type of organization and its activities. For example, if the organization does not have employees, the risks associated with employees will not be present. However, directors ought to keep in mind that individuals retained as independent contractors may be considered by the law to be employees notwithstanding the intentions of the "employer" and the "employee". Whether someone is an employee, dependent contractor or independent contractor is a question of fact. To obtain guidance as to potential liabilities facing a specific organization or

1 This chart is adapted from Canadian Centre for Philanthropy materials prepared in 2001.

arising from particular circumstances, boards or directors should seek a legal opinion based on full disclosure of all the relevant facts pertaining to the organization or situation. Obtaining such guidance from qualified counsel strengthens the argument that a board or director has acted prudently in dealing with the risk.

Also, it is important to remember that while a risk may exist and the potential for liability arises from that risk, unless there are damages that can be shown to be caused by actions or failures to act, a duty of care and a breach of any standard of care, liability does not crystalize. Similarly, the potential for liability may exist even where the organization caused injury to a third party, but there are various defences available before either the organization or its officers and directors will be held to be liable for payment of the damages.

Furthermore, while the organization may be held liable for a breach of contract or tortious act, that liability does not necessarily transfer to the directors or officers, especially where the organization is a corporation. One of the reasons to incorporate is to isolate the directors and members from personal liability for the actions of the corporation that give rise to liability. Indeed, incorporation is a major method to minimize personal risk for the individuals who are directors or members of an organization. Incorporation creates a "corporate veil" which is a shield in most cases protecting against personal liability. The ability of the plaintiff "to pierce" the corporate veil is limited but evolving. It can happen where there is a statutory provision that permits it, where one corporation so dominates and controls another that the second corporation has no real separate mind or existence, or the actions are fraudulent in nature. In the case of employees, for example, most incorporating statutes and employment standards statutes provide for personal liability on the part of directors and officers for unpaid wages and certain benefits, such as vacation pay.

The intention in this chapter is not to review in detail the law of intentional torts and negligence or when a breach of contract occurs; that type of analysis is beyond the scope of this text. Rather, the intention is to identify areas of potential risk so that organizations and their boards of directors and officers are aware of the potential risks and potential for liability and can act to prevent such risks occurring.

Source	Breach	Standard	Duty	Liability	Defence or Risk Management
Incorporating statute	general compliance with statutory requirements; filing requirements; conflict of interest disclosure; inspection of or access to books and records; annual meetings; preparation of financial statements; audits	strict liability; *mens rea* standard, i.e., knowingly, willingly, acquiesced in, authorized, participated in	to comply with the requirements or to cause the corporation to comply	liability will vary depending upon contravention from fines to fines and imprisonment	strict liability offences have a "due diligence" defence; *mens rea* offences require evidence by prosecutor of intention. Appropriate policies and procedures and evidence of compliance and monitoring of compliance could support a due diligence defence. Records may also demonstrate no intention to fail to comply or cause failure to comply with requirements

Source	Breach	Standard	Duty	Liability	Defence or Risk Management
Letters Patent	acting outside scope, i.e., *ultra vires*	unsettled law, potentially that of a corporate director or of a common law/ statutory trustee	exercise care; exercise prudence; exercise due diligence; manage affairs; act in best interest of the corporation; act in good faith; act honestly; act loyally; avoid/ disclose conflicts of interest; non-competition	as corporate directors, liability to reimburse the corporation for any and all losses arising from the carrying out of *ultra vires* activities; as trustees, liability to account for misapplied trust funds regardless of loss or gain that may have occurred	ensuring a copy of the letters patent and any supplementary letters patent are on file and reviewed annually, and that all activities fall within the scope of the letters patent
By-laws	acting beyond the scope of authority set out in the by-laws	unsettled law, potentially that of a corporate director or of a common law/ statutory trustee	exercise care; exercise prudence; exercise due diligence; manage affairs; act in best interest of the corporation; act in good faith; act honestly; act loyally; avoid/disclose conflicts of interest;	as corporate directors, liability to reimburse the corporation for any and all losses arising from acting beyond the scope of the authority; as trustees, liability to account for the misapplied funds regardless of loss or gain that may have occurred	ensuring copies of the current by-laws and resolutions are on file and reviewed at least annually, and that all activities undertaken are authorized by the by-laws and any relevant resolutions

Source	Breach	Standard	Duty	Liability	Defence or Risk Management
Common law duties of directors	failure to act in the best interests of the corporation	requirement to act with the degree of skill that may reasonably be expected from a person of like knowledge and experience	exercise care; exercise prudence; exercise due diligence; manage affairs; act in best interest of the corporation; act in good faith; act honestly; act loyally; avoid/disclose conflicts of interest; non-competition	liability for losses arising from failure to meet standard of care or from breach of duty; liability to account for breaches of fiduciary duties (failing to act in good faith, failing to act in the best interests of the corporation, failing to disclose and/or acting in conflict of interest)	exercising due diligence in preparation for, and taking of, all decisions; procedure for directors to declare interest and recuse themselves from decisions; taking all decisions on the basis of the best interests of the corporation
Common law and statutory duties as a trustee or akin to a trustee	breaches of trust, *Trustee Act* or, in Ontario, *Charities Accounting Act*	requirement to act as a reasonable and prudent person would in the management of his or her own affairs	exercise care; act reasonably; act gratuitously; keep accounts; non-delegation; prudence; diligence; good faith; honesty; loyalty; avoiding conflicts of interest/ self dealing	liability to account for misapplied trust funds regardless of loss or gain occasioned, or to account for breach of duty; removal as a trustee/director	exercising due diligence in preparation for, and taking of, decisions; policy of no remuneration of directors for services (except with court approval); treatment of assets as objects of a trust, rather than merely corporate holdings

Source	Breach	Standard	Duty	Liability	Defence or Risk Management
Trustee's duty re investing the trust assets	improper use or investment of monies or other assets	requirement to exercise the care, skill, diligence and judgement that a prudent investor would exercise	exercise care; act reasonably; act gratuitously; keep accounts; non-delegation; prudence; diligence; good faith; honesty; loyalty; avoiding conflicts of interest/ self dealing	liability to account for misapplied trust funds regardless of loss or gain occasioned, or to account for breach of duty; removal as a trustee/ director	exercising due diligence in preparation for, and taking of, all decisions as to use or investment of charitable property; policy of no remuneration of directors for services (except with court approval); treatment of assets in accordance with the requirements of the *Trustee Act* – N.B.: the Act permits the delegation of some trustee responsibilities provided that the delegation is within the parameters set out in the Act; it also provides relief for certain technical breaches

Source	Breach	Standard	Duty	Liability	Defence or Risk Management
Taxation and related statutes, e.g., *Income Tax Act*, *Employment Insurance Act*, *Canada Pension Plan Act*, *Excise Tax Act* (GST), *Retail Sales Tax Act*	failure to remit source deductions (income tax, CPP, EI); failure to remit GST or retail sales tax collected; failure to submit or forward payment; tax evasion	strict liability; knowingly or *mens rea* standard, i.e., knowingly, willingly, acquiesced in, authorized, participated in	duty as director or trustee	liability for amounts owing plus any interest and penalties; in some cases, fines and/or imprisonment	exercise due diligence, which could include requiring certificate from senior staff that source deductions were remitted and that any taxes collected were remitted; policies and procedures (including audit procedures) that document compliance with the law
Regulatory statutes, such as *Competition Act* and consumer protection statutes; environmental protection, employment standards, occupational health and safety, and labour relations and pension benefits statutes, human rights legislation, and regulatory statutes for area of activity, e.g., day care	failure to comply with standards established by or under the statutes; contravention of any offences, e.g., unfair business practices, polluting waters	vary according to statutory provision from strict liability to *mens rea* standard. In some environmental and health and safety statutory schemes, absolute liability may exist	as director and/or trustee	fines and/or imprisonment; civil liability for any damages caused by breach of standards to injured persons; orders to remedy or correct problems	strict liability offences have a "due diligence" defence; *mens rea* offences require evidence by prosecutor of intention. Appropriate policies and procedures and evidence of compliance and monitoring of compliance could support a due diligence defence. Records may also demonstrate no intention to fail to comply or cause failure to comply with requirements

C ROLE OF INDIVIDUAL DIRECTOR IN MANAGING RISK

I. Overview of Duties

Officers and directors are subject to both common law and statutory duties. As the chart above illustrates, these duties are far-reaching and the standard of care, potential for liability and the approaches to managing the risks vary tremendously in each situation. When combined with the wide variety of activities that charitable and not-for-profit organizations carry out and the differences in staff experience and competence, it is clear that there is no simple statement that is applicable to all organizations and all directors.

There is a general expectation that boards, each director and each officer will take care, act with prudence, act reasonably, and will be informed about the issues that are before them. Directors and officers need to be diligent and knowledgeable about the organization and its operations. There is both a statutory and common law obligation for the directors to manage the affairs of the corporation and, in the case of unincorporated associations, there is a common law duty to do so. Directors must always act in the best interests of the organization and not on behalf of a particular interest. The requirement to act in the best interests of the corporation is paramount regardless of the fact that the director may obstensibly be elected or appointed as a representative of an interest or other organization. In such circumstances, the director may bring a perspective informed by his or her previous experience or background to discussions or decision-making, but is not permitted to place other interests before those of the organization of which he or she is a director. Where the director is faced with interests at odds with each other, he or she should withdraw from discussing or deciding is faced with interests at odds with each other, he or she should withdraw from discussing or deciding the matter at issue.

Directors and officers have fiduciary duties to the organization. These duties require them to act honestly, to be loyal and to act in good faith. They are also to avoid conflicts of interest and not compete with the organization or exploit its opportunities. If a conflict of interest does arise, the minimum expectation is full disclosure and that the individual will not participate in any decision on the matter. To whom full disclosure is made is sometimes an issue — for example, some conflicts of interest are based on very private and personal information. By-laws sometimes provide for disclosure to a designated person, such as the chair of the board. However, the incorporating statute must always be complied with in any such disclosure.

If the director is a trustee or "akin to a trustee" in the case of charitable organizations, the fiduciary duties and standards go further. The directors must act gratuitously and may not accept benefits from the corporation. The directors may be reimbursed for expenses actually incurred, but no more. A director cannot, for example, be a consultant to the charitable organization. This restriction makes it clear that any self-dealing is also not permitted and places a very high burden on directors to avoid conflicts of interest. As a trustee, a director must be impartial and cannot act for a specific interest or group. There are also restrictions on what may be delegated to others, such as investment decisions for the trust property.

It is not really clear in law to what extent directors of charitable organizations are "trustees" or "akin to trustees".[2] It is probably best for any individual director to avoid being the one who is the subject of any court decision that clarifies the issue. If the director of a charitable organization acts in accordance with the standards expected of a trustee, he or she will likely avoid any problems. Indeed, directors of not-for-profit organizations may want to act in a similar fashion for most situations.

Due diligence is an important concept in issues of liability. Liability is less likely to arise where directors have been informed and behaved appropriately and ensured that decisions are thorough and well-documented. How to do so will vary. Generally, the courts do not look for perfection but rather whether the director acted with due diligence as opposed to cavalierly or without regard to the impact of decisions (or a failure to decide). Risks can, therefore, be reduced if the board is well informed, there is a full and frank discussion of the matter before the board, the board makes its decision, that decision is well-documented and supported, the decision is within the scope of its permitted activities under the letters patent, and the decision is made in accordance with the by-laws, rules of procedure or order, and any statutory requirements.

In some cases, decisions or a failure to make a decision will give rise to criminal or quasi-criminal offences. It is impossible to participate in modern life without running the risk of regulatory offences — statutory or similar schemes at the federal, provincial or municipal level. Indeed, in

---

2 For a good critical review of the case law and position taken by the Public Guardian and Trustee in Ontario on this issue, see B.J. Burke and W.I. Innes, "New Developments and Selected Issues in the Liability of Directors and Officers of Charitable and Non-Profit Organizations", in *Fundamental New Developments in the Law of Charity in Canada* (Toronto: Canadian Bar Association – Ontario, Continuing Legal Education, October 27, 2000).

some cases, with privatization, the offences may be in legislation that is enforced by the private sector.

There are not a lot of cases involving charitable and not-for-profit organizations for regulatory or criminal offences. What is clear from those cases is that there is no "get out of jail free" card for charitable or not-for-profit organizations. What difference does it matter to the environment whether the polluter is a charity or a business? There may be a different approach to sentence because personal profit was not a motive, but the issues of punishment, rehabilitation, specific deterrence and general deterrence apply no matter who committed the offence.

It is probably safe to say that every organization commits some offence at some time during its existence. People, including honest people who act in good faith and are diligent, make mistakes. But has the board of directors minimized the risk of mistakes and the contravention of a regulatory statute through education of directors, officers, staff and volunteers? By the adoption of appropriate policies and procedures? Through monitoring and compliance programs? By taking appropriate action when a problem arises? By preventing future contraventions? These types of activities will both minimize the risks and help to illustrate that the organization and its directors and officers are sincere and made a mistake as opposed to knowingly breached the law or were negligent and cavalier in their actions.

II. Checklist for Directors

Directors should endeavour to fulfill the following:

- always act with a view to the best interests of the organization;
- understand and comply fully (in spirit and letter) with the conflict of interest policy;
- be informed about your organization's mandate, its constating documents (letters patent, trust deed, memorandum of association, by-laws) and its incorporating statute if incorporated;
- discuss matters that are before the board fully and with frankness and candidness;
- actively avoid conflicts of interest and, where a conflict arises, disclose the conflict and do not participate in the decision;
- exercise due diligence, care and skill in carrying out responsibilities as officer or director;
- fulfil fiduciary duties of good faith, honesty and loyalty;

- get independent or outside advice where it is required to ensure that decisions are well- informed;
- ensure effective internal monitoring and reporting systems are in place, including for financial matters but also in areas where there is high risk or regulatory requirements;
- attend meetings and, if not available, ensure you are informed about the issues and decisions through minutes and agenda items and any required follow-up;
- keep abreast of the organization's activities and how those activities fit within mandate and its strategic plan and annual plan;
- ensure that the resources are available or become available to implement decisions;
- monitor compliance with statutes and regulations, especially those that regulate directly the fields in which the organization operates, e.g., day care;
- never forget that the role of the director is to manage the affairs of the organization;
- obtain confirmation that source deductions (taxes, EI, CPP and other pension benefits) have been remitted and that any taxes collected on behalf of governments are remitted;
- prepare adequately for all board and committee meetings;
- question whether the matters being discussed are within the mandate of the organization and the decision is authorized by the by-laws;
- state any concerns or objections clearly and ensure they are recorded in the minutes, especially if there is a reason to believe there may be a contravention of the law or there is a risk of liability;
- test treatment of assets against the standards of what a reasonably prudent person would do in comparable circumstances if he or she were dealing with his or her own assets — which may be a higher standard than what individuals actually do with their own assets
- examine your own performance objectively and determine if you meet your expectations of what a good director does or ought to do.

Nobody is perfect; but that statement cannot excuse a director from making an honest and good faith effort to meet their legal and moral obligations. Evidence of good faith goes a long way to satisfy a court and regulators.

D BOARD MANAGEMENT OF RISK

I. Accountable Boards

If the role of the board of directors is to manage the affairs of the corporation, including managing risks; and if boards make decisions at meetings, the logical place to start any discussion about boards and management of risk is at the board meetings. The first step towards management of risks is to ensure that the board meetings operate effectively, efficiently and within the law.

An effective board of directors or trustees is a major method to prevent problems from occurring and, as a result, to minimize the potential for personal liability. The success or failure of an organization is also dependent in large measure on the board being effective. The overall purpose of the board is to manage the affairs of the organization. In doing so, the board provides direction to the organization to permit it (through staff, volunteers and agents) to carry out its objects and to ensure that the organization meets its legal obligations, maintains its status and is financially responsible. The board is to plan how the organization will carry out its objects, to use the resources available to it, and to manage any risks.

The board should, in carrying out its responsibilities, allocate specific functions and tasks to specific individuals. Those individuals as president, vice-president, treasurer, secretary (or whatever other title is used) are accountable to the board for the performance of those functions or tasks.

Boards often operate through committees, both standing and *ad hoc*, for membership, budget, audit, fundraising, human resources, volunteers, special projects, strategic planning and so forth. The types and numbers of committees should reflect the needs of the organization and permit it to carry out its objects in an effective and efficient manner. Terms of reference should be prepared and adopted for each committee, including membership on the committee. It may be useful, for example, to have non-board members on the committee. However, it is important to recall that committees are generally advisory only. It is the responsibility of the board of directors to manage the affairs of the corporation. The committees ought to provide advice and/or carry out the directions of the board.

It is also important that the committees not become a parallel or duplicative accountability mechanism for staff, confusing the lines of accountability. If staff report to the executive director and the executive director reports to the board or a committee of the board, that is the line of accountability. There is a danger if committees assume that staff report to them alone or in addition to the executive director. This may occur more often where the committees parallel staff functions or departments. The risk is probably greater with a "policy governance" board because of the natural inclination of people to want to get involved. Directors in this situation should curb their inclinations.

Much as people may dislike meetings, it is at meetings that matters are discussed, issues debated and decisions made. Modern telecommunications make it easier for directors to meet while physically in different places. Legislative amendments have permitted, for example, meetings to be held through conference calls and in some cases through the internet.

II. Policies and the Prevention and Minimization of Risk

a) What are Policies?

Boards make decisions, but do not always implement them in person. One way to ensure implementation is to put in place policies that must be followed by staff, volunteers and agents in carrying out their respective duties. A policy is a governing principle.[3] It allows the board to delegate to others (staff, volunteers or agents) the authority to act on behalf of the organization, but does so in a way that maintains the board's control. Essentially, it establishes the framework on what is to be done. Policies are often philosophically based, providing a brief statement of the board's views or approach on the matter. It may set out beliefs, values and desires. A policy allows staff, volunteers, agents and others to know what the board wants and expects and why.

Usually, a policy will identify the direction but leave the methods to those implementing the policy. However, this need not always be the case. As discussed in Chapter 1, there are different approaches to governance — the "policy governance" and "administrative governance". There is no right or wrong approach. In reality, most organizations will (or ought to) find a comfortable and appropriate place along the spectrum between the two approaches — which place may move as the organization matures, undergoes stress or change in senior staff, or adapts to a new environment.

There is another factor that mediates against full acceptance of the "policy governance" approach. Volunteers want to do good, which is why

---

3 See M.A. Paquet, R. Ralston & D. Cardinal, *A Handbook for Cultural Trustees: A Guide to the Role, Responsibilities and Functions of Boards of Trustees of Cultural Organizations in Canada* (Waterloo, Ont.: University of Waterloo Press, 1989) at 28 to 29.

they volunteered in the first place. Directors are no different in this regard than any other volunteer. It is very difficult to get personal satisfaction on an ongoing basis from having adopted a good policy on some matter. Those who developed the policy may obtain a higher level of personal satisfaction, but merely approving a policy after some discussion does not usually make one's heart flutter with happiness. People want — and will — attempt to participate in decision-making whenever they can. Not to recognize this factor ignores the human dynamic in organizations.

On the other hand, this factor also mediates against adopting the full "administrative governance" approach. Policies are intended, among other things, to bring a reasoned approach to a particular matter or issue. They also assist in bringing consistency and overall fairness to decisions. They encourage (or should encourage) full consideration of all relevant factors before a decision is made on the merits of any particular matter. Indirectly, a policy will also carve out areas of responsibility so that those who know and do the job best are the ones who have the responsibilities to do so. Directors will be discouraged from getting involved in decisions for which they bring little or no expertise, knowledge, understanding or value.

This factor leads one to another purpose of policies — accountability. If the policy identifies who is to do what, when and what results are expected, then the policy also provides a basis for evaluation of the "doer" and for accountability. The staff or volunteer should know what is expected of him or her and he or she can be assessed against that standard.

b) Policies Governing the Board

The board is also subject to "policies". These policies are more process, planning and decision making in nature. Traditionally, they have not always been seen as policies and have been called by other names. For example, a basic policy that all organizations must have are by-laws, which set out who does what, when and often how. By-laws will cover such matters as financial affairs, record-keeping, timing of and conduct at meetings and so forth. Yet too often boards will forget about, or even worse, not be aware of the by-laws.

Policies are also set out in resolutions of the board. These resolutions may set up committees or identify methods by which the board will operate. The resolutions may prescribe certain approaches to issues or document how certain decisions are to be made or even what the decisions will be in similar situations. For example, a board that decides on who gets a scholarship or bursary may set out by resolution what the eligibility criteria will be for applicants to be considered. Several of the policies have already been discussed in previous chapters. For example, the strategic plan is an essential policy that will govern resource allocation, partnerships and so forth for the organization.

What types of policies ought to be in place or considered? Context, obviously is important to answering this question. If the organization does not have employees or volunteers, there is no point in having human resource policies. There are a number of possible policies for most organizations:

- Governance Policies

  - letters patent, memorandum of association, trust deed or similar constating document;
  - by-laws;
  - organizational structure or chart, especially if the organization is larger and has employees. This chart should set out decision-making levels so that it is clear who (or what position) makes what types of decisions. A "job description" for each position would also assist in making clear who does what;
  - board structure, including executive committee and its role and responsibilities, standing and *ad hoc* committees and their terms of reference and lines of accountability. Often, this information will also be in the by-laws and may be required in some cases. For example, for corporations in Ontario, if there is an executive committee that will make decisions, it must also be referenced in the letters patent;
  - rules of procedure or rules of order at meetings;
  - conflict of interest policies, either as a separate document or as part of a code of conduct for directors;
  - communications policy, both internal and with outside stakeholders. This policy could include advocacy;
  - access to information and privacy policy. This area of policy is becoming increasingly important as a result of legislative changes and an increased focus on privacy in a wired world. Clearly, organizations that have employees or who provide social services will have a greater need for a policy in this area than an organization that puts on the occasional play.

- Strategic Planning

    - mission statement that is based on the letters patent or other constating document;
    - statement of goals and objectives;
    - business plans.
    - budgets and resource allocations based on plans

- Operational Policies

    - financial management, such as cash management, internal procedures, banking arrangements, internal audit;
    - compliance management to demonstrate compliance with significant regulatory requirements that face the organization;
    - human resource management, which would include policies with respect to workplace and sexual harassment, hiring, promotions and retention, volunteer management, training, discipline and conflict of interest (including use of the assets of the organization, such as computers);
    - program management, which will include review of programs to ensure that they are meeting their objectives. The programs ought to include overall assessment criteria so that it is easier to determine if and when a program is successful or requires further adjustment, refinement, resources or elimination.

Several components of the governance policies, including strategic plans were discussed in Chapters 1 and 2. These policies are the basis upon which the organization carries out its mandate and, indeed, defines its mandate from a legal perspective (what its constating documents permit it to do) and from a priorities and resource allocation perspective (what its strategic plan, annual plan and budgets provide is to be done). Others will be explored in other texts in this series, including one on human resource management and financial management and will, as a result, be briefly identified and discussed. This chapter will review the internal governance policies and identify issues that ought to be addressed in policies, review some policies that are increasingly important to charitable and not-for-profit organizations and set out some sample policies.

c) Policy Process

The development of policies and their approval, implementation and evaluation are separate but integral components in the policy process. The following checklist is intended to assist in the process, but it is not "the final word". Policies need to flow from the strategic plans of the organization, its legal obligations and what it can do from a practical perspective. A legitimate use of a policy is to minimize risks. However, if the policy is so sophisticated and resource intensive that it is not followed, it may instead lead to increased risk because the organization did not follow its own policy on the matter and that failure caused, directly or indirectly, injuries to another person.

The size, nature and level of sophistication of an organization, its context and the expertise of its staff (if any) need to be taken into account in how any such policy process actually works. The overall "governance approach", i.e., policy governance or administrative governance, will also be an important factor in how the board addresses the policy process. In any event, the following elements could be included in a policy process:

- identification of a need for a policy, which may include a corporate policy to review all policies on a periodic basis or to require senior management to do so and identify areas that require new policies or revisions to existing policies;
- terms of reference for the committee or person who is to prepare the draft policy, including membership, time allocated for the preparation, consultation and so forth. In many cases, it is probably desirable to include staff and senior staff representation on the committee or, at least, consult with them. A committee may also need to retain external expertise, such as a lawyer, accountant or management consultant;
- format to be used for policies, in particular where consistency is desired for clarity purposes;
- research into the policy issue, assessment of current situation and its risks, need for policy and the proposed content of the policy. The research should also examine what options are available with respect to the policy and how any policy proposal will inter-relate with other policies and the overall mandate of the organization;
- review of any legal requirements or standards that are applicable;
- drafting of policy for review and comment, including any background materials that will assist the board in making a decision on the

proposed policy. The board may want to consult on the draft policy, in particular where internal and/or external input have not been provided;

- discussion of the draft policy and preparation of final version;
- development of an implementation plan, which may include communications with staff and volunteers and with external stakeholders, training, allocation of resources for implementation, scheduling of activities, allocation of responsibilities and determination of who is accountable for implementation;
- approval of the policy and implementation plan and any related requirements, e.g., resource allocation;
- evaluation of policy after a prescribed period to determine if it is effective and addresses issues.

The policy ought to identify clearly what the issue is, the goals for the policy, the fundamental values or beliefs being advanced by the policy and how they relate to the mandate of the organization. It should also identify who is responsible for the policy and its implementation — both initially and on an ongoing basis.

d) Internal Governance — By-Laws and Rules of Procedure or Rules of Order

1 BY-LAWS

By-laws are a fundamental governance policy. As with the constating documents, the board will normally not make changes or cause changes to be made without the approval of the membership. Technically, the board enacts the by-laws and any amendments to them and they will usually be effective as of that date. However, the by-law or amendment requires the approval of the membership for them to continue to be effective after the annual general meeting. Normally, subject to exceptional circumstances, the board would propose changes to the by-laws and allow for the members to comment, if not provide explicit approval.

The by-laws can contain much of what is typically included in "governance policies" and items that go to the pith and substance of an organization. For example, the by-laws will usually include provisions on:

- membership qualification, limits on numbers, classes of membership, resignations, expulsion or suspension of members, *ex officio* members;

- board of directors and number, election, removal, remuneration (if permitted by law), *ex officio* directors;
- board meetings, including notice, quorum and minutes;
- officers and their duties, election, removal, remuneration (if permitted by law) and *ex officio* officers, such as past president;
- committees, including executive committee (if permitted by law), standing committees, functions and membership and appointment of *ad hoc* committees;
- members meetings, including procedures for calling and conducting annual or general meetings, special meetings, notice requirements, agendas and so forth;
- indemnification to directors, officers and others;
- execution of documents;
- voting, voting methods and majorities required;
- proxies (if permitted);
- banking, auditors, financial year, books and records, custody of books and records (financial and secretarial);
- fees, dues and assessments;
- procedures to amend the by-laws;
- rules and regulations;
- adoption of rules of procedure or rules of order.

A number of the provisions in by-laws will, therefore, cover matters that could be included in governance policies that are developed by the board. If the by-law provides for the matter, it would take precedence over any "policy" approved by the board that is inconsistent. Indeed, depending upon how detailed the by-law is, the by-law may occupy the field and severely restrict any supplementary policies.

This situation is neither good nor bad. It may express the desires of the membership that the board be restricted in how it decides to operate and make decisions. Organizations that are small, for example, may prefer that the board be tied into a consultative approach to making decisions. If that approach is set out in the by-laws, the board is obliged to follow it and cannot change that approach without referral back to the members.

2) RULES OF PROCEDURE OR RULES OF ORDER

The board may need policies on its own internal operations. Not all of these will be contained in the by-laws or in strategic plans. These policies are more procedural in nature, often called rules of procedure or rules of order. They set out how decisions are to be made. Typically, an organization will adopt rules of procedure. There are several different versions of these rules.[4] However, it is questionable whether the adoption of such rules of procedure is the best approach. The adoption of *Robert's Rules* or similar rules of order is made by reference in a by-law but without any thought as to the appropriateness for the organization. Simpler rules of procedure that are developed in the context of the organization are preferable, where the time can be devoted to preparing them. And too often nobody knows what the Rules say because a copy was never actually obtained.

Rules of procedure or rules of order — either as provided for in the by-laws or in separate rules of procedure or rules or order — will cover the following matters:

- election or appointment of chair. The election or appointment of the chair for the meeting and any substitute or temporary chair, and the removal or vacating of the chair;
- duties of chair. The duties of a chair are significant and occur before, during and after any meeting. The chair needs to be aware of and knowledgeable about the organization's constating documents, by-laws and the rules of procedure. The chair will normally prepare or cause to be prepared notice of the meeting and an agenda for the meeting. The chair should also ensure that the accommodations for the meeting are appropriate for the anticipated attendance and that any appropriate amenities are available, such as refreshments.

  During the meeting, the chair is to call the meeting to order, ensure that the meeting is properly constituted and that those in attendance have a right to be there. He or she will ensure that notes are taken, which will be used for the preparation of minutes.

  The chair is also responsible for conduct during the meeting. Meetings are productive only if proper order is maintained. However, balanced against the need for order is the need for open and full discussion of issues and a recognition that, at times, tempers can flare and passions can arise. A chair needs to enforce decorum in a

---

4 For example, G. Standford, *Bourinot's Rules of Order*, 4th ed. (Toronto: McClelland & Stewart Inc., 1995); J.M. Wainberg & M.I. Wainberg, *Wainberg's Society Meetings Including Rules of Order* (Don Mills, Ont.: CCH Canada Ltd., (1991); H. Perry, *Call to Order: Meeting Rules and Procedures for Non-profit Organizations* (Burlington, Ont.: Big Bay Pub., 1984); A. Beauchesne, *Beauchesne's Rules and Forms of the House of Commons* (Toronto: Carswell, 1978); *Robert's Rules of Order Newly Revised*, 10th ed. (Cambridge, Mass.: Perseus Publishing, 2000); A. Sturgis, *Standard Code of Parliamentary Procedure*, 3rd ed. (New York: McGraw-Hill Inc., 1988); or M. Mitchell Cann, *Robert's Rules of Order – Simplified* (New York: Perigin Books, 1991).

responsible, even-handed and reasonable way. He or she should insist on discipline and respect for opposing views and, if necessary, adjourn the meeting to bring order back. If somebody becomes excessive, the chair has a duty and a right to expel that person from the meeting.

The chair also has a duty to act fairly, in good faith and without malice. Although tempers may flare, the chair needs to remain calm and collected. The chair decides who will speak when and for how long (subject, of course, to any express rules otherwise). The chair should keep the meeting moving along and on agenda, whenever possible. At times, an agenda item will take longer than anticipated and adjustments need to be made. The chair may canvas the meeting on this point or make an assessment and decision on his or her own.

As noted previously, boards make decisions, which are documented. The usual method of making and documenting a decision is by resolution which is recorded and voted upon. Resolutions are made by motion, which is seconded, discussed or debated, and voted upon. The chair should consider the wording of the motion to ensure that it is appropriate (not disrespectful or substantially the same as one that has already been dealt with) or out of order because it is contrary to the law or the organization's constating documents. A motion could be made before discussion occurs or after an issue has been discussed. Often, the appropriate action to take comes to light only after a full and frank discussion has occurred. In any event, the chair has a role to ensure that the discussion occurs, to determine when sufficient discussion has occurred, to determine the sense of the meeting and to call for a vote and declare the results.

The chair may or may not have a vote. Some organizations prohibit the chair of the meeting from voting, others provide a vote to the chair and a casting vote (second vote in case of a tie), or a vote only if there is a tie (which is different from a casting vote where the chair votes twice because the tie occurs without the chair's vote) or only has a vote as do others. Normally, for a motion to pass, the motion must receive a majority of the votes. The by-laws, constating documents or incorporating legislation may provide that certain matters require a two-thirds or other majority. In any event, if the vote is tied, usually the motion fails. The chair also declares when the meeting is ended. Usually, there will be a motion to end the meeting.

The chair usually cannot move or second a motion or amendment while acting as chair. It may be possible for the chair to temporarily vacate the position to do so. Some rules provide that the chair may move or second a motion when only one other person is present who is qualified to do so.

The chair normally should not discuss the merits of a motion. However, human nature makes this restriction very difficult to enforce. It also depends upon the culture of the organization. A chair may, however, want to vacate the position if he or she will be taking a strong or controversial position on the subject. It is also not uncommon for chairs to participate more fully in a meeting if the meeting is a board meeting or committee meeting where the sense is that it would be appropriate. An annual general meeting or public meeting is different from the monthly finance committee meeting.

After the meeting, the chair is responsible for ensuring that the minutes are prepared. Often the secretary is designated to prepare the minutes by the by-laws or otherwise. However, the chair has a responsibility to ensure that the minutes are prepared and accurately reflect the meeting. There are several approaches to minutes — they can be a very detailed, blow-by-blow report of the meeting or simply a record of who attended, who was absent and what decisions were made, or anything in between;

- appeals from chair. Some rules of procedure provide for appeals from procedural rulings of the chair. Normally, these appeals are not necessary but an appeal process may be appropriate for some organizations. If there is an appeal process, there will be an obligation to follow it in a fair manner. The appeal could be to those in attendance at the meeting or to the board. If there is to be an appeal process, the process should clearly identify what could be appealed, when and under what circumstances. It should be done immediately at the meeting or as soon as possible to another body such as the board, require a second, not be open to debate (other than brief statement of reasons for the appeal and a response by the chair) and be voted on. In rare circumstances, somebody could apply to the courts and if this process is intended to be available, it should be noted in the rules. These provisions would be very unusual in procedural rules for the board's decision-making process.

- quorum for meetings. Quorum requirements are typically set out in the incorporating legislation and/or in the by-laws of the organization, but the rules may sometimes repeat the quorum requirements or refine them. Normally, quorum is not less than two-fifths of the positions on the board of directors, i.e., if the number of positions of directors is ten, quorum will be at least four. If the number of positions is 11, quorum would be five. Quorum could be higher than two-fifths, such as a majority or even more, but practical experience will provide some guidance. A higher percentage may encourage more directors to attend, otherwise they will feel guilty if quorum is not reached and no decisions can be made. On the other hand, an excessively high quorum will lead to frustration as quorum is not reached and those in attendance have wasted their time. If the constating documents do not state what quorum is, it is generally taken to be the majority of positions.

Recent changes to legislation and policies have permitted directors to attend through conference call or similar telecommunications methods. All boards ought to consider using this technique not only for quorum purposes but also to encourage a full participation in meetings at least cost to those involved. Whatever the method used, each person must be able to clearly hear each other, otherwise, the conditions of having a "meeting" will not be present.

A few issues arise from quorum. Are *ex officio* directors included or not? If the *ex officio* director does not have voting rights, is he or she still part of quorum? What about honorary directors? If these individuals have voting rights and rights to attend and participate at meetings, arguably they are part of quorum. This fact is sometimes overlooked in preparing by-laws that allow for *ex officio* directors. What happens, for example, if the mayor of a municipality is an *ex officio* director but never attends the meetings? If the by-laws are silent on the matter, decisions taken at the meeting may be subject to challenge if achieving quorum turned on the *ex officio* director's attendance.

Some organizations also are unclear about who is included in quorum. If there are nine positions of director but only seven are filled, and quorum is a majority, is quorum five or four? Quorum in this case would be five as quorum is based on the number of positions, not the number of positions filled. A majority of nine is five. Again, lack of clarity could leave scope for decisions to be challenged.

Another issue that periodically arises is what happens if quorum disappears? This can occur especially where a meeting is lengthy. Unless the constating documents or by-laws provide otherwise, if quorum disappears, no further business may be transacted at the meeting. It is common, therefore, to provide that once quorum is reached, quorum will be maintained for the remainder of the meeting. On a related issue, quorum will be deemed to continue regardless until somebody raises the issue. If no quorum count is taken or demanded, quorum once reached is presumed to continue. Query, however, if there are only five members out of the nine and the quorum-making director leaves. Arguably, the chair may have an obligation to raise the issue of quorum.

If quorum is lost and the by-laws do not permit quorum to continue, what happens? Or if quorum is never obtained, can the meeting continue? Yes and no. There is nothing necessarily wrong if those in attendance discuss the issues, provided that it is understood that no business may be transacted. It may be possible for those in attendance to take a position on the matter, which can be brought to the next board or committee meeting. That meeting's notice and agenda would include the item, any motions that were developed and so forth and, the subsequent meeting could transact the business;

- motions present a wealth of opportunities for weird and wonderful things to occur. The rules should provide for types of motions and when they may be made. Several types of motions are recognized in rules of procedure. These include:

  - main motions, which are substantive in nature. These motions will direct or authorize somebody to do something, or adopt, ratify, approve, confirm or reject something that has been done. They can also be used to express the opinion of the meeting or of the organization. A main motion should be seconded before it is open to debate. If it fails to be seconded, it does not go to the next step. Main motions may be amended (which may be a friendly amendment that the mover accepts) or unfriendly. If unfriendly, the amending motion ought to be debated and voted upon first before the originating motion is voted upon or debate is continued on it;
  - amendment motions, which are intended to amend motions and resolutions;
  - subsidiary or procedural motions, which address the conduct of motions. A procedural motion takes precedence to an amendment motion or the original main motion. Procedural motions may deal with objections to the matter being considered, or state that the matter be put to a vote immediately, that discussion or debate be closed or postponed, or that the motion

be referred to another committee or be referred back to the initial committee, or that the rules be suspended;

- motions to close, recess or to adjourn the meeting. An adjournment may be to a fixed date or a date to be scheduled; and
- motions for the election or appointment of directors, officers and similar positions.

Different rules of procedure or rules of order will use different classes of motions and may also categorize them in varying ways. In some rules, a motion to amend is a subsidiary motion, as are motions to table a motion, to close, limit or extend debate, to postpone to a definite or indefinite time, or to refer to a committee. Incidental rules are those that involve appeals to the chair, points of order, procedural inquiry or information, suspensions of the rules, withdrawal or modification of a motion and so forth.[5]

Statutes sometimes also require that certain by-laws or changes to the constating documents may only be made by "special resolution" requiring a two-thirds majority. Certain matters may also be raised as motions but are more in the nature of a demand or privilege. For example, if somebody is questioning whether or not quorum is present, a quorum count may be requested. There may also be points privilege (personal or general), points of information or of procedure or of order that may arise. The more formal the rules of procedure, the more likely these types of motions or points will be covered.

Typically, rules of procedure will provide that only one motion may be on the floor and open to debate and vote at any given time. This procedure ensures that people have a better chance of knowing what is being debated and what the vote is for.

Motions should be informative and form the basis for debate or discussion and a vote. A motion will include the subject under discussion. It should be within the power and scope of the meeting and the organization's lawful authority. Motions should be affirmative, not offensive or argumentative. Historically, motions have had words included, such as "whereas" but these words are not required. Indeed, the fewer the words and simpler the language, usually the better. Motions that do not comply with the rules are to be ruled out of order.

---

5 Contrast, for example, the classification used in *Robert's Rules of Order – Simplified* with that in Standford's *Bourinot's Rules of Order*.

Motions require a seconder. If no seconder is willing to do so, the motion dies. However, this rule has been a matter of convention and is not for the most part a legal requirement. Indeed, many of the rules of procedure or rules of order are based on conventions that have developed over the years — some of which may no longer be relevant in the twenty-first century or to the organization. The chair can second a motion if there is no other eligible person to do so. The secondment of a motion is really a test of whether or not there is any interest to debate the matter.

Motions may be divided, especially if there is more than one proposition in the motion which can stand or fall independently of the others. For example, a motion to support something in principle could be divided from a motion to support something in principle and to provide funding for it at that time. A motion to divide the main motion must be seconded. It cannot be amended and is debated solely on the issue of dividing the main motion. The debate and vote on any motion to divide a main motion is done before debate or a vote continues on the main motion. If there is more than one motion to divide, each is taken in turn until one is acceptable. Any remaining motions to divide are not followed up as the division has already been made.

A motion may also be withdrawn by the mover before it is seconded or the chair states it. After that point, the motion is in play and the meeting will decide its fate — to permit the withdrawal on consent of the meeting, to be deferred, to be voted on or otherwise considered. A motion to withdraw is like any other motion and requires a seconder. It is not open to amendment and is not debated.

Amending motions are useful to allow the meeting to consider alternatives to the motion that is currently before the meeting. There may be several amendments to substantive motions as the meeting considers different approaches or wording. But each amendment must be dealt with in turn — including any subamendments to an amendment to a substantive motion. On contentious matters, the number of motions, amendments and subamendments (including those designed to kill or neuter the original substantive motion) can multiply and try the skills of the chair. The chair needs to keep things moving and to ensure that proper order and procedure are followed for fairness. However, at some point, proper order also means bringing matters to a conclusion.

The essence of meetings and motions is to promote discussion and debate of issues with a view to a decision or resolution. Openness is particularly key for not-for-profit and charitable organizations because of the nature of their mandates. With the advent and widespread public popularity of the *Charter of Rights and Freedoms*, Canadians have become more conscious of issues like "free speech" and "due process". An organization can rarely do itself harm by allowing full and frank discussion of the issues it faces, though admittedly this process can, at times, be taxing. But a far greater danger lies in stifling debate, which can hurt not only the organization itself but also reflect poorly on the voluntary sector as a whole. Canadians pride themselves on the democratic principles set out in the *Charter of Rights and Freedoms*[6] and in other constitutional and legal documents. The terms "free speech" and "democracy" are sometimes used during meetings and board meetings of organizations. Canadians are inculcated with the concept and it has become bred to the bone.

Discussion or debate should generally be open. However, the chair needs to ensure that no one person or group of persons so dominate a meeting as to hijack it. A debate by its nature means that more than one viewpoint is put forth and considered. Some people become intimidated or are too shy to speak their minds. Opportunities should be made to ensure that all persons can express their views in a fair and full manner. Once that view is expressed, it is common practice to limit any further discussion by the same person until after all others who want to speak have had the opportunity to do so. The chair can also limit any supplementary discussion by a previous speaker to responses to new information or points of view, and not permit an ongoing repetition of the same information or opinion. Similarly, if the same view is being expressed repeatedly by a series of speakers, the chair may want to consider limiting any further comment to new perspectives or for new information. While speakers have a "right" to speak it is a constrained one.

The concept of the "floor" is an important one in promoting an orderly debate or discussion of an issue. People should be recognized by the chair before they speak, especially in larger meetings. It may be less formal in smaller meetings — and, indeed, the culture of the organization may mitigate against formalities such as putting up one's hand to be recognized. Speakers deserve a fair opportunity to make their points in a concise and forthright fashion without fear of heckling, undue interruption or disruption. A speaker could be interrupted, for example, on a point of order or procedural matter. Once that matter is dealt with, the floor returns to that speaker, assuming of course that the point of

---

[6] Part I of the *Constitution Act, 1982*, being Schedule B to the *Canada Act 1982* (U.K.), 1982, c. 11.

order or procedural matter did not result in him or her no longer having the floor.

There are several procedural motions that may arise in relation to a substantive motion. For example, somebody may object to the substantive motion on the grounds that the action contemplated is illegal, contrary to the organization's constating documents, repetitive, unwise, not needed or for other reasons. The individual may bring a motion to object to the consideration of the substantive motion. This motion must be brought at the time the agenda is being reviewed or when the substantive motion is brought and before another speaker starts on the motion. This type of motion does not require a seconder because it is more in the nature of a demand that any requirements for the motion to be dealt with be met.

There are also a variety of privileges that may be considered at a meeting. For example, an individual who feels that he or she has been insulted or subjected to abuse may raise a point of personal privilege. A point of general privilege may also be raised if, for example, the speaker cannot be heard, or the room is uncomfortable or too crowded. A point of information may be raised if the information is being provided in good faith and is not intended to divert the discussion or to be argumentative. Finally, points of procedure may be raised, provided they are raised in good faith and are not argumentative. A point of order may also be raised if the agenda is not being followed or there is a similar irregularity. All of these demands or privileges are to be considered immediately before ongoing debate of a motion continues.

There are a number of very good rules of procedure or rules of order. An organization may adopt one of them or it may develop its own rules. The above discussion was intended to canvas the major issues that are covered in such rules and to identify some matters that have been and will be in the future contentious. Whatever "policy" for meetings is selected by the board, the overriding principle is that it should be fair and allow all members an opportunity to participate in the discussion of an issue and to do so without any fear or abuse. The role of the chair is crucial and, as a result, the chair must remain as neutral as possible. He or she needs to understand the sense of the meeting and, at times, be courageous to ensure that there is a proper balance of "free speech" with effective and efficient decision making.

E SELECTED POLICY DOCUMENTS

There are a number of policy areas that have become or are becoming particularly important in the governance of charitable and not-for-profit organizations. These policies have developed either from legal requirements or from a consensus around the need for such policies. The remainder of this chapter will examine policies for conflict of interest of directors; the collection, use and disclosure of information; financial management and regulatory compliance management; and indemnification and insurance. In Chapter 4, policies with respect to the management of the "assets" of the organization are reviewed, including investment policy, human resources and organizational structures.

1. Conflict of Interest

Conflicts of interest are inevitable. The very people that most organizations want to attract to their boards and to be active as officers or chairs of committees are the ones most likely to be active elsewhere in the community. They have interests that are varied — both in the sense of things that are of interest to them and in the sense of interests with which they are involved. The issue in any conflict of interest policy is to ensure that any legal requirements are being complied with and that the policy is reasonable.

There will be commonality of elements in any conflict of interest policy in the sector. However, charitable organizations will generally have more stringent policies because of the influence of the law of charity. The issue of whether or not the director is a trustee or akin to a trustee raises its head again with respect to conflicts of interest. In Ontario, there are particular issues that arise from the positions taken by the Public Guardian and Trustee, such as the purchase of insurance.

If the organization is a corporation without share capital (not-for-profit), the incorporating legislation usually addresses at least one form of conflict of interest. Section 98 of the *Canada Corporations Act*[7] and section 71 of the Ontario *Corporations Act*[8] provide statutory processes for a director to disclose and deal with a situation in which a director has a direct or indirect interest in a contract with the corporation or that is proposed. The director has a duty to disclose his or her interest at a meeting of the board of directors. If the contract is proposed, it shall be

---

7 R.S.C. 1970, c. C-32.

8 R.S.O. 1990, c. C.38.

declared at the meeting at which the question of entering the contract is first taken into consideration or at the next meeting if the director is not at that meeting. If the director becomes interested in a contract after it is made, the declaration is to be made at the first meeting of directors held after the director becomes so interested. However, nothing stops the director from making an earlier disclosure.

The director could also make a general disclosure that he or she is a shareholder or otherwise interested in any company or a member of a firm and thereby has an interest in any contract to be made with that company or firm. It may be appropriate, though, for the director to remind his or her colleagues of this fact should a contract or proposed contract arise. A declaration made several years ago may not be immediately remembered or the various interconnections of businesses may not be readily apparent from the general disclosure.

The director is not permitted to vote in respect of any contract or proposed contract in which he or she has a direct or indirect interest. If the director does vote, that vote is not to be counted. There are some exceptions under the federal legislation, such as contracts by or on behalf of the corporation to give to the directors security for advances or by way of indemnity, if there is no quorum of directors in office who are not so interested, and the director holds shares in the other business only to qualify to be a director or officer of that corporation.

If the director has complied with the statutory provisions on conflict of interest, he or she will not be held accountable to the corporation for the contract or proposed contract by reason only of holding the office or of the fiduciary relationship established for any profit realized by the contract. If the contract is confirmed at a meeting of the members called for that purpose, the director will also not be liable.

In the case of the Ontario statute, there is also an offence under subsection 71(6). If the contract was voidable only by reason of the director's interest, he or she is liable upon conviction to a fine of not more than $200. While this fine is not large, it does indicate the seriousness with which this type of conflict of interest is held.

The statutory provisions would not appear to apply as readily to charitable corporations, where the directors are seen to be trustees or akin to trustees. Any interest, direct or indirect, would appear to be prohibited. There are obvious difficulties with such an iron-clad position. For example, would it prohibit a director from renting a facility operated by the charitable corporation for a family event? For a business event? If the director has shares in mutual funds and the mutual fund holds shares in a business that contracts with the charitable corporation, is there a conflict of interest? At some point, the rubber band of conflict of interest becomes too stretched to make sense. While the director could always bring an application to the court to remedy any such "breach of trust", it seems ludicrous to do so where the contract is not material. If there is doubt as to the contract being material the director may want to obtain a legal opinion — a cost which is to be borne by the director and not the organization.

There are other complications that may arise, which indicate a need for further reform of the law in this area. If the corporation without share capital has a charitable object but is not exclusively charitable, what are the rules? Is it sufficient for the director to comply with the statutory provisions? Or does he or she need to comply with the "charitable" requirements? Does it matter if the contract is not concerned with the charitable assets? Or can the charitable assets really be so easily divorced from the analysis?

A conflict of interest policy should have the following elements in it. A sample conflict of interest policy is included in Appendix I to illustrate how those elements could be articulated.

- definition of what a conflict of interest is. This definition should incorporate the legal requirements in any incorporating statutes, such as personal interest in a contract. The issue of family relationships may also be relevant for some organizations. For example, a director may be the spouse, parent or child of another director or of an employee of the organization. Or the family member may have an interest in a contract with the organization, either as a supplier of goods or services or as somebody who receives goods or services from the organization. The issue of receipt of goods and services may be relevant in many organizations. For example, directors are usually members of the organization. Could directors receive the same discount on tickets for a production as do other members? Could they rent the organization's clubhouse for a personal event just as any other member?
- what information must be disclosed about a conflict of interest? This factor may be very sensitive. If a director is in a personal relationship with somebody, that information may be very sensitive. Or the conflict may arise out of a confidential business dealing. On the other hand, without full disclosure of information, it is not possible to assess whether or not a conflict of interest does exist and, if it does, how to address the conflict. Not all conflicts necessarily lead to resignation; there are many steps in between that could be

considered, including removing oneself from the decision making process and having no participation in the discussion of the matter;

- to whom must the information be disclosed? It may not be necessary or appropriate to inform everybody about the conflict or the facts surrounding the conflict. Many organizations have a staged process, whereby a director discloses to the chair the conflict and the relevant factors. The chair or director may inform the board of the existence of the conflict and how it has been resolved. In other cases, the board may need to know more about the conflict, especially where the integrity of the board or its decision or decision making process is at stake. In addition, if the director has a personal interest in a contract, most incorporating statutes set out a procedure to address that type of conflict;
- range of remedies to address a conflict. As noted above, resignation is one remedy but recusing oneself is another. The remedies will be influenced by whether or not the organization is not-for-profit or charitable. The nature of the conflict will also affect the type of remedy that may be available. The remedies should also consider the materiality of the conflict. Some conflicts are trivial; others are fundamental;
- penalties for breach of the conflict of interest policy. Although this element is related to remedies, it assumes that there has been a failure (deliberate or otherwise) to comply with the policy. For example, what is to happen to a director who knows that he or she has a conflict, does not disclose and benefits personally as a result? The board may want to consider having the corporation take legal action against that director if the matter is sufficiently serious, in order to protect the corporation and their own integrity;
- disclosure of information to members. In some cases, it may be appropriate to disclose the conflict to members at the annual general meeting. This approach may also be mandated by incorporating statutes with respect to material contracts. An auditor may also need to know about any such material contracts as part of the audit of the financial statements.

Conflicts of interest may be real or they may be perceived. They may be actual or potential conflicts. Where a conflict has not occurred but the director is aware that there is potential for it to occur, the director may want to disclose or at the very least avoid any involvement with the issue. The board and director should also consider public and member perception of conflicts of interest. There may, in fact, be no conflict of interest because the director has arranged his or her affairs to avoid any. However, a reasonable person could still perceive a conflict to exist, based on the information that is available to him or her. He or she may not know or have access to relevant information about how the conflict was avoided. These types of conflicts will probably need to be dealt with on a case by case basis, but the board needs to be aware of perception in how it deals with conflicts.

There are also some built-in conflicts. For example, if *ex officio* directors are appointed, as discussed earlier, conflicts may develop that are inherent to why the person is a director. Similarly, people may be directors because of a broader interest in the community. They are directors because of involvement in related matters. If so, care must be taken to avoid conflicts.

II. Code of Conduct

A code of conduct is another useful policy to regulate the behaviour of the directors. It allows directors to understand their roles and the limits to those roles. It also assists in ensuring that meetings and activities are carried out in a civil manner, with a view to making appropriate decisions in a timely manner.

A code may include the conflict of interest policy. Or it could be separate to emphasize the importance of both policy areas. In any event, a code of conduct could include the following matters:

- "job" descriptions for the director and for the officer positions;
- information about the organization, its programs, strategic plans and so forth;
- expectations that the board has of all directors, including those related to fundraising (which may include personal donations), community relations, contributions of time, work on specific committees or projects (such as policy development);
- requirement that directors prepare for, attend and participate in meetings of the board and of the relevant committees. The code could establish a minimum standard for attendance which if not met could trigger a review of that director's ongoing appointment;
- lines of accountability and what the director may or may not do with respect to staff;
- information on the essential policies of the organization and agreement to comply with those policies, including workplace harassment and discrimination;

- criteria for assessing whether or not the director is doing a good job as a director. This topic could be expanded to include the board's evaluation of its collective performance;
- behavioural guidelines, such as act in the best interests of the organization, comply with the principles of fairness, act in a civil manner, when acting on behalf of the board in public to do so with integrity, duty to participate fully and frankly at meetings, maintain confidential the confidential business of the board and so forth.

Codes of conduct can be used to reinforce the objects of the organization as well as the duties that directors must meet.

III. Personal Information and Privacy Policies

Organizations collect and use personal and other information as part of their activities. Different types of organizations will, obviously, collect varying amounts of information. The degree of sensitivity of the information may also vary from organization to organization or within an organization. A social services agency that delivers care to the elderly, for example, will have access to very personal and sensitive information, much more so than a community theatre group that usually only needs to know addresses and past experience in theatre.

Similarly, an organization that has employees will collect personal information, some of which will be very sensitive. How sensitive that information is may be dependent upon events beyond the control of the organization. For example, the address of an employee in normal circumstances may not be very sensitive and can usually be located in the telephone directory. But it is easy to envision situations in which the employee will not want others to know where he or she lives.

An organization may also need to collect information about its volunteers. If the volunteer is working with children, youth, the elderly or vulnerable people, the type of information may be very personal. An organization that provides services to children, for example, may want to know whether the volunteer has any convictions or findings of guilt for criminal offences. That type of information is obviously sensitive but necessary to safeguard the child and the organization.

A word about "criminal records searches": the typical criminal records search is not as informative as most people think. Typically, the individual will either obtain the records search or authorize the organization to obtain it. This authorization is required because the records are subject to confidentiality provisions in federal and provincial legislation and contractually as between law enforcement agencies in Canada. The search will normally provide information about convictions in the previous three years. What will likely be missing from the search document obtained by the individual or the organization are any findings of guilt (absolute or conditional discharges where the conditions have been met), charges that were not proceeded with for substantive or procedural reasons, peace bonds and any convictions for which a pardon has been given. What certainly will not be included are any police intelligence information. Also, these records are only as good as the information that has been entered into the computer system. If, for whatever reason, the information about a conviction was not entered, it obviously will not be on the search document.

The search is not comprehensive in other ways. If the volunteer is to drive children or others to sports events or medical appointments, the volunteer's driving record would certainly be relevant information. Does the volunteer have a practice of driving too fast? Or not signal when making turns? Or drive without insurance? Or drive while the licence is suspended? The criminal records search will not likely provide any of this information unless it is tangential to a criminal conviction or resulted in criminal charges and conviction. Requesting a copy of the driver's licence will not tell the organization whether or not it is suspended or was cancelled for non-payment of fines. Yet, in many situations, this information will be of more practical assistance to an organization in protecting itself and those under its care than information about a 20-year-old conviction for shop-lifting as a teenager.

There has been, in recent years, substantial pressure on all institutions in Canada to protect personal information and to justify the collection, use and disclosure of such information. Federal legislation, which will govern throughout Canada unless similar legislation is enacted in a province, is the most recent example of this pressure. Although it does not apply fully to charitable and not-for-profit organizations, it would be a mistake for these organizations to ignore the legislation and the public sensibilities behind it. In addition, the statute will apply whenever certain information is transferred across provincial borders. Provincial legislation may also go beyond the federal legislation, which will place even greater pressures on organizations to comply with the law and the spirit of the law.

The *Personal Information Protection and Electronic Documents Act*[9] is intended:

> to establish, in an era in which technology increasingly facilitates the circulation and exchange of information, rules to govern the collection, use and disclosure of personal information in a manner that recognizes the right of privacy of individuals with respect to their personal information and the need of organizations to collect, use or disclose personal information for purposes that a reasonable person would consider appropriate in the circumstances.[10]

The Act applies very broadly to organizations that collect, use or disclose personal information in the course of commercial activities, or if the personal information is about employees and the organization uses the information in connection with the operation of a federal work, undertaking or business.[11] Few charitable or not-for-profit organizations would fall within the second part of section 4, dealing with federal work, undertaking or business. However, the legislation includes a provision that contemplates the Act applying to provincial transactions (where there is commercial activity), at a future date if substantially similar provincial legislation is not enacted before that date. Although this provision may be subject to challenge as an infringement on provincial jurisdiction, prudence dictates that organizations assume their treatment of personal information is highly likely to be subject to some form of regulation in the foreseeable future, and put appropriate measures in place. The Canadian Standards Association Privacy Pinciples incorporated in the federal legislation are the recognized benchmark in this area and are likely to be reflected in provincial legislation enacted. Accordingly, they are a good starting point for any organization developing a privacy policy.

"Organization" includes an association, partnership, person and trade union[12] and would, therefore, include most, if not all charitable and not-for-profit organizations. There may be an issue with respect to "trustees" but it is likely that the statutory definition of "organization" is sufficiently broad to include that form.

The critical definition is "commercial activity". That phrase is defined in subsection 2(1) as:

---

9 S.C. 2000, c. 5.

10 *Ibid.*, s. 3.

11 *Ibid.*, s. 4.

12 *Ibid.*, subs. 2(1).

> any particular transaction, act or conduct or any regular course of conduct that is of a commercial character, including the selling, bartering or leasing of donor, membership or other fundraising lists.

It is clear that charitable and not-for-profit organizations will fall within the ambit of the Act if they sell, barter or lease any of these lists. "Personal information" means information about "an identifiable individual". It does not include the name, title or business address or telephone number of an employee of an organization.[13]

But the statute will apply to the personal information collected, used or disclosed by an organization for other commercial activity. One of the ambiguities in the Act is the applicability of the requirements to revenue-generating transactions carried on by not-for-profit or charitable organizations in fulfilment of their mandates. For example, would the Act apply to a community theatre that collects the home address, e-mail address, telephone number and opinions of patrons about a show? What if the community theatre wanted to use that information to add the patron to its mailing list for upcoming productions? Would it matter if the community theatre is "in competition" with a for-profit commercial theatre in the community? Or if the community theatre organization is going to add the patron to its list for fundraising purposes?

What about a charity that operates a store to sell used clothing? Is that a commercial activity? Could it collect and use information about its customers? Would the type of use matter, for example, if the store employee collected information to confirm the identity of a patron who is paying by cheque? Could that same information be used to add the patron to the mailing list for upcoming specials? Or to the fundraising list?

If the organization participates in any revenue-generating activity, it is likely that personal information collected in connection with this activity will fall within either the federal or provincial legislation (if enacted). Where provincial governments enact legislation it could even apply in circumstances where there is collection of personal information unrelated to commercial activity (at least one province has contemplated developing privacy legislation of general application rather than triggered by commercial or revenue-generating activity). Accordingly, organizations and their boards ought to be evaluating their collection and treatment of personal information with a view to putting in place protocols that will comply with present or future privacy legislation.

---

13 *Ibid.*

Section 5 of the Act requires that every organization shall comply with the obligations set out in Schedule 1. That schedule is based upon the CSA International's *Model Code for the Protection of Personal Information.*[14] The obligation to do so begins in 2000 (2001 for health-related information) for federally-regulated organizations and for the international and inter-provincial trade in personal information, and in 2004 for organizations that operate solely within a province. If the relevant province enacts comparable legislation, then the organization is exempt from the federal legislation but must comply with the comparable provincial legislation. The exemption, though, will only apply to intra-provincial transactions. The federal Act will continue to apply to any international or inter-provincial trade in personal information.[15]

The CSA International *Model Code* has ten principles, which are followed by a number of notes. The ten principles are set out below. After each principle, a possible "policy" is provided. None of these sample policies is intended to be the answer for any particular organization; rather they are there to illustrate how an organization can meet its legal requirements. Different organizations will have different needs.

- Accountability — An organization is responsible for personal information under its control and shall designate an individual or individuals who are accountable for the organization's compliance with the following principles.
  ABC is responsible for personal information of its members, employees and donors under its control. The board of directors has appointed a chief privacy officer who is accountable to the board and reports directly to the chair of the board on ABC's compliance with this privacy policy.

- Identifying Purpose — The purposes for which personal information is collected shall be identified by the organization at or before the time the information is collected.
  ABC will identify the purposes for which personal information is collected by us at or before the time the information is collected. An individual can choose not to provide all or some of the personal information to ABC that is requested. However, where the information is required to provide the services or is legally required to be collected (for example, to issue a receipt for income tax purposes), ABC will decline to provide the services. The

---

14 CAN/CSA-Q830-96.

15 Section 30, S.C. 2000, c. 5.

individual will be informed so that he or she may decide whether or not he or she still wants the services and will provide the information required.

- Consent — The knowledge and consent of the individual are required for the collection, use or disclosure of personal information, except where appropriate.
  The individual's knowledge and consent are required for the collection, use or disclosure of personal information. ABC will only collect or disclose personal information for purposes that are appropriate under the circumstances or to comply with any other legal requirements.

- Limiting Collection — The collection of personal information shall be limited to that which is necessary for the purposes identified by the organization. Information shall be collected by fair and lawful means.
  ABC will only collect personal information that the board has determined is necessary for the purposes identified by ABC. Information will be collected only in accordance with the law. The board has reviewed and will review annually the specific purposes for which personal information is collected from its members, employees and users of its services.

- Limiting Use, Disclosure, and Retention — Personal information shall not be used or disclosed for purposes other than those for which it was collected, except with the consent of the individual or as required by law. Personal information shall be retained only as long as necessary for the fulfilment of these purposes.
  ABC will not use, disclose or retain personal information for any other purpose than for which it was collected, except if the individual has consented or it is required by law. ABC will not sell, rent, barter, exchange or otherwise deal membership, donor or other fundraising lists. ABC will only disclose to third parties personal information where the individual has consented to such disclosure or ABC is required to do so by law.

- Accuracy — Personal information shall be as accurate, complete and up-to-date as is necessary for the purposes for which it is to be used.
  ABC shall keep personal information as accurate, complete and up-to-date as it can. Information about members shall be confirmed annually as part of the member's annual renewal. Information about employees shall be confirmed each year as part of the employee's performance appraisal. Records shall be corrected or updated within five business days of notification of the error or update.

- Safeguards — Personal information shall be protected by security safeguards appropriate to the sensitivity of the information.
  Personal information will be kept in a manner that is secure having regard to the sensitivity of the information and other legal requirements. Sensitive personal information shall be kept in a locked cabinet and, in electronic format, shall be accessible only by an authorized user. Access to sensitive information shall be tracked using sign-out sheets and, in electronic format, through password access in accordance with the privacy procedural manual.

- Openness — An organization shall make readily available to individuals specific information about its policies and practices relating to the management of personal information.
  ABC *shall provide to individuals a copy of its policy on privacy and make available a summary of its procedural manual.*

- Individual Access — Upon request, an individual shall be informed of the existence, use and disclosure of his or her personal information and shall be given access to that information. An individual shall be able to challenge the accuracy and completeness of the information and have it amended as appropriate.
  An *individual may request in writing access to information being held by* ABC. ABC *will inform the individual of the existence, use and disclosure by* ABC *of any personal information. The individual will be provided access to that information, provided such access is not prohibited or restricted by law. If the information is not accurate or complete, the individual may provide the correct or complete information and the changes shall be made where the changes are substantiated.*

- Challenging Compliance — An individual shall be able to address a challenge concerning compliance with the above principles to the designated individual or individuals accountable for the organization's compliance.
  Challenges concerning compliance by ABC *with its privacy policy may be made to the chief privacy officer, whose decisions shall be final. The chief privacy officer shall inform the chair of the board of the context of any such challenge and the resolution, but shall not disclose to the chair the name of the challenger unless it is necessary to do so in the circumstances.*

The *Model Code* includes lengthy notes for each of these principles. Unfortunately, the Act includes a number of modifications to the *Model Code* and those notes,[16] which makes it difficult at times to assess the impact in any particular fact situation. The federal Privacy Commission has prepared a more detailed analysis and guide to the *Model Code* and the statute to assist businesses and organizations to identify and meet their legal obligations.[17]

The Act also gives the Privacy Commissioner a role in the handling of complaints. The Commissioner may investigate a complaint under section 12 of the Act and has substantial powers to carry out the investigation. For example, the Commissioner may summon and enforce the appearance of a person before the Commissioner and compel him or her to give oral or written evidence on oath and to produce any record or things that the Commissioner considers necessary to investigate the complaint. The Commissioner may also attempt to resolve complaints.

Complainants have a number of possible remedies. The Commissioner is obliged under section 13 to prepare a report that sets out the Commissioner's findings and recommendations, any settlement that was reached and, if appropriate, a request that the organization give the Commissioner notice of any action taken or to be taken to implement the recommendations, or reasons why not. Subsection 13(2) authorizes the Commissioner not to issue a report in certain specific circumstances where other remedies or procedures are available, the complaint is too dated, or the complaint is trivial, frivolous or vexatious or made in bad faith. Under section 14, a complainant may, after receiving the Commissioner's report, apply to the Court for a hearing into the matter. The Court has broad powers to issue an order under section 16, including to correct the practices in order to comply with the Act and to award damages. Finally, the Commissioner may also carry out audits on organizations under sections 18 and 19 of the Act.

The Act is a strong disincentive to organizations to sell, barter or lease their membership, donor or other fundraising lists — if that is the only "commercial activity" under which the organization would fall. If they intend to do so, they must comply with the *Model Code*, as it is amended by sections 6 to 9 of the Act. The organization would need to obtain the consent of the individuals to disclose the information, which may be

---

16 Sections 6 to 9 set out a number of modifications, which should be read in conjunction with the Schedule.

17 *Your Privacy Responsibilities: A Guide for Businesses and Organizations to Canada's Personal Information and Electronic Documents Act* (Ottawa: Privacy Commission of Canada, 2000). It is also available at the Commission's website – privcom.gc.ca.

difficult to do after the fact. If the organization intends to sell, barter or lease its lists, it should obtain the express permission to do so in advance. And it should set up its systems in a manner that allows it to comply with this legislation.

There are some issues that need to be resolved. Could chapters of a national organization exchange their lists? It is not clear from the legislation that they could without complying with Act. This situation may cause difficulties for some national or inter-provincial organizations that share their lists for mutual benefit.

Organizations may also fall under the Act if they carry on other forms of commercial activities. For example, if the organization carries on a business activity, it would need to comply with the Act if it uses the information in more than one province. This compliance may be an extra cost of business that the organization cannot justify.

There is another important but less easily understood impact of the Act. It has raised the bar for charitable and not-for-profit organizations. Increasingly, donors and prospective donors will come to expect organizations to comply with the federal or provincial requirements as a matter of course. Charitable and not-for-profit organizations should consider compliance in areas in order to meet the developing expectations of donors and prospective donors.

Equally important, employees of organizations will come to expect compliance with the *Model Code* whether or not strict compliance is required by law. All employers owe common law duties to their employees and former employees to maintain personal information confidential and to use it only for *bona fide* purposes. But with the codification of "rights" into the *Model Code* and its use as a basis for legislative enactment, it can be expected that employees will demand a more rigorous protection of their rights. Volunteers are also likely to have similar expectations. And all of these expectations are growing at the same time as the need to "screen" employees and volunteers increases to avoid liability from inappropriate employees or volunteers.

IV. Financial Management Overview

The board should establish some level of financial overview of the affairs of the organization either as a board function or a committee function.[18]

[18] See Price Waterhouse, *Fitness Test for Corporate Directors*, Toronto, undated. Although this guide was prepared for directors of business corporations (and larger ones) it is a useful one for directors of charitable and not-for-profit organizations. The basic obligation for financial management does

The level will depend upon the size and sophistication of the organization. The level of review, for example, need not include detailed analysis of the procedures used by management unless there have been problems with those procedures. The board or a committee may assess the integrity of the internal controls and information systems of the organization but it would leave the day-to-day monitoring to management.

Typically, in larger organizations, a committee of the board will be responsible for the ongoing overview of the finances of the organization. An "audit committee" is often established for that purpose and is recommended by the Panel on Accountability and Governance in the Voluntary Sector. This committee would be responsible for the financial affairs of the organization, at the initial stage, and accountable to the board in that regard.

The board's policy on financial overview would be set out in the terms of reference for the audit committee. The terms of reference for an audit committee could include the following:

- review of the accounting principles and their application to ensure that they are appropriate. If any changes are proposed, review any changes that may have a material impact on current or future years. In doing so, it is important to consider the reasons for the change and the views of the organization's auditor on the changes;
- consider whether or not the accounting policies and procedures being used are similar to those used by others in the sector and, if not, why not;
- review significant accounting policies that may be controversial or that may have recently been addressed by the CICA or others. In some cases, funding agencies may suggest certain accounting policies or approaches to be consistent with their own requirements; in other situations, it may be that Canada Customs and Revenue Agency has identified issues or a new matter has arisen;
- review the use of the deferral or restricted fund accounting method and, in particular, ensure that the method used is carried out properly and is consistent with providing the most useful information;

---

not change because one is a director of an organization as opposed to a director of a business. The director remains accountable and, as part of a board, responsible for the management of the affairs of the organization.

- review any significant litigation, claims or contingent liabilities with a view to ensure that they are properly disclosed and that appropriate provisions are being made where possible to cover them;
- review any differences of opinion between management of the organization and the external auditor and consider how to resolve such differences of opinion;
- review any material adjustments that have been made to the financial statements by the external auditor and understand why they were made;
- compare operating results on an ongoing basis to previous years and to budget, and satisfy self as to why there are differences or deviations;
- review interim financial statements or financial forecasts on a quarterly or monthly basis;
- review with the external auditor his or her involvement and any issues that arise;
- review management's suggestion for external auditor and the terms of engagement, including audit fees;
- review circumstances in which a material misstatement could occur in the financial statements and the planned audit steps to prevent any misstatement;
- determine the role of the external auditor in other matters in the financial management process, i.e., preparation of the financial statements;
- determine if the auditor should be involved in any "compliance" audit activities, such as compliance with the board's policies or with internal control mechanisms;
- meet with external auditor and make sure coordination is present with internal accounting or audit staff;
- review and follow-up on any auditor's recommendations and management's responses;
- review internal audit arrangements, such as the terms of reference for internal audit;
- assess whether or not the internal audit staff are competent, objective and qualified;
- review and approve the budgets for internal audit;
- review the results of any internal audit reports and management's responses. If necessary, resolve any disputes.

V. Regulatory Compliance Management

The board has a role to ensure that any regulatory requirements are complied with in the operations of the organization. It may do so as a board or through a committee that reports to the board, such as the audit committee or a compliance committee. What those regulatory requirements are and how they will be monitored will depend upon the activities of the organization and its status. For example, corporations are obliged in their incorporating statutes to maintain certain books and records. The responsibility for doing so will lay with either the treasurer or the secretary, depending upon the by-laws and the nature of the books and records. The secretary will normally also be responsible for any corporate information filings, and the treasurer, any financial filings, such as the charity information return by registered charities with Canada Customs and Revenue Agency.

There will be other regulatory requirements that are applicable to all entities or in certain sectors of the economy. For example, all employers have legal requirements to collect and remit income taxes and certain other employment-related taxes and premiums for employment insurance and Canada Pension Plan. A failure to do so can result in charges against the officers and directors and in personal liability. A board of directors will want to put in place measures to avoid such liability. Similarly, there may be environmental laws that apply to the organization. These may apply generally or as a result of the activities of the organization.

If the organization is involved in activities that are specifically regulated, it will need to comply with any such regulation. Most health care providers are regulated. Many social service agencies are regulated. These regulations may arise either directly by statutes or indirectly through contractual obligations. For example, an organization may agree by contract to comply with certain standards in the delivery of services.

The variety of regulatory obligations is too great to provide a one-size-fits-all policy. However, certain elements ought to be included in a regulatory compliance policy:

- identification of regulatory measures that apply to the organization. This identification could be done by class:

    - requirements that arise out of generally applicable legislation, such as the *Competition Act* or consumer protection legislation;
    - requirements of incorporating legislation and from constating documents;

- requirements as an employer, such as employment standards, occupational health and safety, human rights code, the *Income Tax Act* and similar statutes;
- environmental laws that apply, including those that are applicable at the federal, provincial, municipal or conservation authority levels. If the organization owns property, there is a higher likelihood that environmental issues will arise but almost all organizations will use property and, in doing so, may cause damage to the environment;
- if a charity, requirements that are unique to charities, such as those under the *Income Tax Act* with respect to books and records, receipts for income tax purposes and, in Ontario, with respect to the *Charities Accounting Act* and *Charitable Gifts Act*;
- requirements that arise from specific sectoral regulations, such as in day care or nursing homes;
- requirements that may not be statutory but are industry standards. For example, although community theatres are not regulated, there are industry standards that apply for health and safety;
- requirements that may be set out by CSA International or other standards setting bodies. In some cases, these bodies may also provide accreditation;
- requirements that are set out in contracts, including funding agreements.

There will be other sources of requirements and the listing of relevant and applicable requirements may be very daunting — especially if there has not been ongoing regular activities in that regard. The first step in the policy process may be simply to get a complete list of these requirements or at least a list of where the requirements are located.

- priorizing of the requirements based upon relevance, potential damage should the requirements not be met and assessment of risk. Not all requirements are equally important. It is essential to determine which ones are more important to the organization than others;
- identification of who is responsible for ensuring compliance with the requirements. Clearly, staff and senior staff will have substantial responsibility for ensuring that there is compliance. However, certain officers may also be responsible, such as the treasurer for financial matters, the secretary for corporate records and filings and so forth.

The key is to have in place the correct person who has the skills, status and resources required and will be accountable for doing so;
- identification of what information is to be provided to the board or a committee of the board with respect to compliance. In some cases, the information may be periodic, e.g., quarterly reports, or where an incident occurs;
- identification of what information is to be provided to senior management with respect to compliance;
- identification of the format that the information will be provided in. It may be that the board will want the executive director to prepare a certificate stating that all income taxes and employment-related premiums have been collected and remitted to Canada Customs and Revenue Agency and the appropriate provincial ministry;
- identification of what internal control mechanisms and quality control mechanisms will be place to ensure that the information is accurate and complete;
- identification of what will be subject to internal or external audit, including a compliance audit where appropriate;
- allocation of responsibilities for follow-up on any deficiencies;
- allocation of resources and to whom in order to implement policy on regulatory compliance management.

Each organization will need to determine for itself and in its own context how to handle regulatory compliance management. However, there may be useful examples within the organization's sector or industry standards that are applicable. The policy needs to be reasonable and rationally based. The board also needs to keep in mind that the information provided must be relevant, timely and useful. There are also some practical matters; the organization is intended to carry out activities. Regulatory compliance is important, but the resources devoted to compliance and compliance management need to bear a relationship to the risks involved, the chance of the risk occurring and the need to carry out the mandate. When in doubt, the board ought to consult or have management consult with the regulator or contracting party to ensure that the compliance management policy will meet everybody's needs.

Chapter 4

MANAGING THE ORGANIZATION'S ASSETS

A INTRODUCTION

An organization can only carry out its activities and fulfil its objects if it has assets with which to do so. Protecting your organization's assets is as important as generating them. The often considerable energy devoted to fundraising efforts or obtaining clients or contracts can be easily wasted through poor management of organizational resources.

Organizations have both tangible and intangible assets. It is important not to overlook the value of intangible assets: public opinion research conducted in 2000 found widespread trust in charities[1] and a strong belief that charitable organizations understand the needs of the average Canadian better than government.[2] While this support does not necessarily always translate into concrete resources, it speaks clearly to the need for organizations to protect their images and reputations. In part at least, success in maintaining the goodwill currently enjoyed by many organizations turns on properly managing, and being seen to manage properly, more tangible assets. However, the importance of goodwill also suggests a need for care in handling matters like volunteer relations, which are apt to be ignored when determining an organization's value.

Thus, the board should take a broad approach to what an "asset" is. Physical assets such as land and buildings, equipment, cash, accounts or grants receivable and supplies are key to carrying out the organization's mandate. But other assets that the board needs to consider and manage

---

1 M. Hall, L. Greenberg & L. McKeown, *Talking About Charities: Canadians' Opinions on Charities and Issues Affecting Charities* (Edmonton: Muttart Foundation, 2000) at 24. Similar research on not-for-profit organizations is unavailable.

2 *Ibid.* at 5.

include intellectual property, information (such as donor lists), employees, volunteers and even the board members themselves.

This chapter reviews the management of these assets from a policy perspective. Each board of directors will need to develop its own approaches and policies with respect to the management of assets. These approaches and policies need to be reviewed periodically to ensure that they are still relevant and appropriate to the circumstances in which the organization operates.

A central, overriding purpose of the management of assets is to ensure that the assets are used in an efficient and effective manner to fulfil the objects of the organization. Assets may only be used for activities and purposes that fall within the organization's objects, as set out in its constating documents. While this legal restriction applies to both not-for-profit and charitable organizations, the boards of charitable organizations are faced with a greater expectation on them that they will ensure that the objects are used solely for charitable purposes. Because the assets are impressed with a charitable trust, the directors have duties that are either trustee in nature or akin to being a trustee.

On this point, it is likely that the courts would take a narrower view of what an asset is for charitable purposes than this chapter takes. For example, it is doubtful that a court in reviewing the actions of a board of directors would consider volunteers of an organization or employees to be impressed with a trust. Nevertheless, this factor should not negate the need for boards to manage volunteers and employees and to deal with them appropriately and with fairness. There are also legal obligations on the part of directors with respect to employees in particular, but also volunteers, to ensure safe working conditions that are free from harassment and discrimination. This chapter will examine that aspect of the management of volunteers and employees as "assets".

B INTELLECTUAL PROPERTY

I. Overview

Intellectual property too often gets short shrift in the management of assets. Yet intellectual property may be very valuable to an organization — both the intellectual property that it owns or developed and what it uses that is owned by others.

There are several forms of intellectual property which may be protected pursuant to federal legislation:

- copyright — literary, artistic, dramatic or musical works, including computer programs, performance, sound recordings and communications signals;
- trade-marks — a word, symbol or picture, or combination of two or more of these items, that are used to distinguish the wares or services of one person or organization from those of others in the marketplace;
- patents — new inventions (process, machine, manufacture, composition of matter) or any new and useful improvement of an existing invention;
- industrial designs — visual features of shape, configuration, pattern or ornament, or any combination of these features, applied to a finished article of manufacture;
- integrated circuit topographies — three-dimensional configuration of the electronic circuits embodied in integrated circuit products or layout designs.

There is another category of intellectual property that is not directly protected by a legislative regime. Trade secrets and know-how are forms of intellectual property that are protected by the owner not allowing others access to them — or access is governed by contracts that permit another person to use the trade secret or know-how, but not reveal it to others. The legislative regimes provide protection for specified periods of time — but on the condition that the owner of the intellectual property reveals it to the public. For example, in order to obtain a patent, the person who applies for the patent must disclose the invention. Copyright is slightly different in that there does not need to be a registration of the copyright, but in most cases, the purpose behind the protection is to ensure that only the holder of the copyright may reproduce it.

The federal legislation operates within an international context in which international treaties and agreements attempt to harmonize intellectual property regimes throughout the world. The World Intellectual Property Office is one mechanism through which the laws that apply in Canada are becoming increasingly similar to those in other jurisdictions. This international harmonization has both positive and negative features for charitable and not-for-profit organizations. It can result in broader protection for the intellectual property of organizations, especially in a wired world and the Internet. But it also requires organizations to comply with legal requirements about which the organizations have little knowledge.

For the most part, charitable and not-for-profit organizations will probably not become involved in patents, industrial designs or integrated circuit topographies. Some organizations, such as research institutes, educational institutions and trade associations, may do so. Indeed, the creation of these forms of intellectual property may be a major activity of these organizations. They will, no doubt, have access to the legal expertise required to plan and protect this intellectual property. These organizations may also have detailed plans for the commercialization of the intellectual property, alone or in conjunction with others which are intended to manage the assets. These assets may be very valuable and provide substantial revenues for the organizations through the sale or licensing of the intellectual property.

Where an organization holds such assets, directors and staff should be mindful of the restrictions on use of the revenues flowing from such assets placed on charitable and not-for-profit organizations. The non-distribution provisions of incorporating statutes and limitations on business activities of charities apply notwithstanding what may appear to be a windfall to the organization. Indeed, regulatory agencies are likely to face greater pressure to tightly enforce restrictions if an organization enjoys marked economic success.

However, these situations will not be the norm for most charitable or not-for-profit organizations, which have more modest expectations. Their major forms of intellectual property will arise from copyright and trade-marks, which may be protected through the legislative regimes, and from trade secrets and know-how. There may be some revenue potential, but it is not a fundamental reason for the creation of the intellectual property.

II. Copyright

The *Copyright Act*[3] applies to original works. Copyright in Canada is automatically created in the author of a work, although the author or somebody acting on his or her behalf may register copyright.[4] Copyright is the legal right:

- to copy a work;
- to produce or reproduce a work,
- to permit somebody else to copy or produce or reproduce a work.

---

3 R.S.C. 1985, c. C-42, as amended.

4 See A *Guide to Copyright* (Ottawa: Industry Canada), 2000 for a good review of copyright law. Industry Canada also publishes a number of very useful publications related generally to intellectual property and which are available from its website at cipo.gc.ca.

There may be copyright in literary works (books, pamphlets, poems and other works consisting of text and computer programs), dramatic works, musical works, artistic works (paintings, photographs, sculptures, maps and so forth). The work must be "original" in order for copyright to exist. Copyright may also exist in a performance, a communication signal (such as a television broadcast) and sound recordings.

Copyright is important for three reasons:

- if an organization wants to use in whole or substantial part works created by another person, it must have permission from that other person to do so. Typically, permission is granted in writing by a licence for which a royalty is paid. In some cases, collectives have been established to manage the issuance of licences, to collect the royalties owing and to enforce the copyright holder's legal rights. For example, if the organization wanted to use a song or part of a song in its fundraising campaign, it would need to obtain the rights to do so from the Society of Composers, Authors and Music Publishers of Canada (SOCAN) or a similar rights organization in the relevant jurisdiction. Similarly, if the organization wanted to use a poem or other text, it would obtain the licence from the Canadian Copyright Licensing Agency (CANCOPY) or similar rights organization in the relevant jurisdiction. A failure to obtain a licence and to pay the appropriate royalty may result in legal proceedings against the organization when the copyright holder enforces his, hers or its rights. The organization may also lose its investment in any materials that were created if the court orders the destruction of the materials;

- the author of the work holds the copyright in most cases. The major two exceptions to this general rule are:

    - if the work is created by an employee the copyright belongs to the organization, unless there is an agreement to the contrary. It is important to ensure that the employee is an employee and not, say, an independent contractor or a volunteer;
    - if the work is created by another person under commission to the organization, unless there is an agreement to the contrary. However, for the work to fall into this exception, the organization must have paid consideration for the copyright. To be safe, an agreement for services, such as advertising copy, should indicate that copyright in the product will be held by the organization.

The author of the work may also transfer the copyright to the organization, a third way for the organization to obtain the copyright. Any assignment must be in writing. The author may do so for consideration or as a "gift". If the author is to receive a receipt for income tax purposes, there should be an independent appraisal as to the fair market value of the copyright,

- enforcement of copyright by the organization. Some businesses or others may attempt to use works for which the organization has a copyright. The *Copyright Act* provides the organization with remedies to cause these persons to cease from doing so. The organization may want to take such steps where, for example, somebody is purporting to be acting on behalf of the organization or who is reproducing the organization's materials for their own benefit.

  Generally, copyright lasts for 50 years after the death of the author. The length of the copyright becomes a bit more complicated when dealing with photographs, sound recordings and so forth. Regardless of the medium or the type of work, it is important to clarify who has copyright and whether or not that copyright remains in force before the organization makes use of any work that has copyright.

The author of the work also has common law and by statute "moral rights" in the work, even if he or she no longer has copyright in the work. The moral right prohibits anybody from distorting, mutilating or otherwise modifying a work without the permission of the author if it would be prejudicial to the reputation of the author. Similarly, the moral right prohibits the work being used in association with a product, service, cause or institution in a way that may be prejudicial. The author may "waive" his or her moral rights, but cannot sell them. If the organization intends to use a work that was created for it and for which it holds the copyright, it may want to ensure that it also obtains the waiver of moral rights so that it has the flexibility that it feels may be necessary for fundraising purposes. The waiver may be general or specific in nature. The moral right continues until the copyright expires.

There are a number of works or parts of works in which copyright does not occur. For example, there is no copyright in facts, ideas or news. The copyright does not exist in the idea but in how that idea is presented. Copyright does not exist in materials that are in the public domain, i.e., where the copyright has expired. The usual example for public domain is the works of Shakespeare. There may be, though, copyright in a reproduction of the works of Shakespeare. Copyright also does not exist in names, slogans, short phrases or methods of teaching. There may be, though, an ability to trade-mark certain of these under the *Trade-Marks Act.*[5]

III. Trade-Marks

The registration of a trade-mark is intended to protect the identity of a corporation or organization. The registration provides legal title to the intellectual property. A trade-mark is a word, symbol, design or combination that is used to distinguish the wares or services of one person from those of another. The underlying intention of a trade-mark is that it represents both the provider and the reputation of the provider.

There are three major types of trade-marks:

- ordinary marks — words or symbols that distinguish the wares or services of a specific firm or individual. Many organizations have logos or other marks that distinguish them from other organizations or even businesses;
- certification marks — these marks indicate that a ware or service meets a defined standard. The mark is owned by one person who licences its use by those who meet the defined standard. The Canadian Centre for Philanthropy's "Imagine" mark is an example of a certification mark in this sector;
- distinguishing guise — a product may come in a unique shape or package, which is readily identifiable.

A trade-mark to be registered, cannot be clearly descriptive of the product, deceptively misdescriptive or designate a place of origin. Similarly, words in another language that are descriptive of the product cannot be registered. The proposed trade-mark cannot be confusingly similar to a registered trade-mark or pending trade-mark and may not incorporate a prohibited mark.

A trade name is not automatically a trade-mark. In order to be registered as a trade-mark, a trade name must be used as such. It must be used to distinguish the wares or services provided by that organization from others.

---

5 R.S.C. 1985, c. T-13. See *A Guide to Trade-Marks* (Ottawa: Industry Canada, 2000).

As with copyright, the owner of a trade-mark may have a common law right to use it. However, that common law right may be reduced if somebody subsequently registers a trade-mark. Registration is *prima facie* evidence that the registered holder is the owner of the trade-mark. The registered holder does not have to prove ownership in a dispute; rather the person challenging the registration must prove ownership.

The registration of a trade-mark can be expensive and time consuming. Often, businesses will retain a trade-mark agent to handle the registration process. The registration is valid for 15 years and is renewable every 15 years. The registration also only protects the organization's rights in Canada. Nevertheless, if the organization has developed a distinctive trade-mark it may want to protect the intellectual property in that trade-mark.

An organization, as with copyright, must take care if it uses the trade-mark of somebody else. For example, if the organization wants to show the public that a business is supportive of the campaign by including that business's trade-mark, it must obtain the permission of the business to do so. This should be done in writing with the scope, duration and any restrictions on use clearly spelled out. The organization should consider registering those trade-marks that it owns which it believes will prove valuable to it.

IV. Wasting an Intellectual Property Asset

Copyright and trade-marks are two assets that boards may ignore and, as a result, "waste" those assets. Trade-marks, for example, can be wasted in several ways:[6]

- confusion with pre-existing trade-marks or trade names;
- failure to restrain unauthorized use of trade-marks may result in loss of distinctiveness through similar corporate names, similar charity names, similar logos or similar domain names on the internet;
- confusion in names involving estate gifts, where the donor is no longer around to clarify his or her intentions;
- failure to control properly the licensing of a trade-mark;
- abandonment through lack of use;

---

6 See, for a fuller discussion of the wasting of trade-mark assets, T.S. Carter, *Avoiding Wasting Assets — Trade-Mark Protection for Christian Charities: Checklist and Reference Guide* (May 15, 1997) which is available at carterslawfirm.com/charity/protect.html.

- limitation on a trade-mark right that is exercised on the basis of the common law because the trade-mark was registered by somebody else;
- dilution of a trade-mark through inconsistent use or different application.

Copyright may also be wasted by not registering copyrighted material with the appropriate collective or allowing others to use copyrighted materials without explicit authorization. Any materials should be noted as copyright protected with the © symbol and reserving all rights through the phrase "all rights reserved" on materials. It is not uncommon for organizations to allow other organizations to use their copyrighted materials; that is not necessarily wrong or a bad idea. Mutual cooperation is an important part of the sector. But it is important to protect the asset through registration of copyright where appropriate and by enforcing rights. It is reasonable to require, for example, another organization to note that it is using the copyright material with permission of ABC Charity. Noting permission is important because, regardless of how close or friendly the relationship between the two principal organizations is, the material may later be reproduced by a third party. If this reproduction reflects badly on ABC Charity it will want to have recourse.

Organizations should also consider joining the relevant collectives. The collectives have the resources and staff to enforce copyright more readily than do most organizations. The collectives arrange for the authorized usage of a work in an efficient and effective manner. Organizations, in any event, need to ensure that infringement of copyright is minimized. If it owns the copyright in material, it should register it where that is practicable and enter into assignment or licensing agreements for the use of the copyrighted materials.

It is also important to ensure that the organization has clear copyright to any such materials or, if not, the ownership interests are clearly set out in agreements. For example, as noted earlier, if the materials were created by an independent contractor, the organization may want to ensure that copyright rests with it and not the "creator" through an assignment and waiver of moral rights. The organization may not want to do this in all cases because the assignment and waiver may increase the costs of the materials to the organization. But somebody should make this decision after the appropriate consideration of the issues, including costs and benefits.

V. Trade Secrets and Know-How

Trade secrets and know-how may be important intellectual property for an organization. A trade secret is a common law protection arising out of a fiduciary duty or obligation to act in good faith. Typically, information that is secret is used by the organization in its operations. It could be, for example, the ingredients used to bake butter tarts at a bakery operated for charitable purposes by the organization. The butter tarts may be unique and bring in customers. The bakery provides training opportunities for the poor and raises money to assist those in need. The organization will want to ensure that the butter tart formula is kept secret so that others may not use it and take away business from the bakery.

To do so, it could limit who knows what the formula is and have all of those with knowledge sign documents acknowledging that it is a trade secret and that they will maintain secrecy. If it wants to licence another bakery to make the butter tarts, it could enter into an agreement to send the mixed ingredients or to provide the information about the ingredients subject to secrecy being maintained.

VI. Respecting Rights of Others

There is also a flip side to intellectual property issues. The organization needs to be able to demonstrate that it complies with the laws with respect to copyright, trade-marks, patents and so forth. It ought not to use "pirated" software or copyrighted materials without the permission of the relevant collective or holder of the copyright or pursuant to one of the limited exemptions in the legislation. It should avoid trade-marks that are confusing or similar to those of others. It should not misappropriate or steal trade secrets.

The board of directors will also want to consider to what extent it needs or wants the copyright in materials created by its employees. There may be circumstances in which it is appropriate to allow the employee to have an interest in the copyright. Boards should consider what intellectual property could be commercialized and how to do so. These types of issues may be important for boards if the organization produces significant intellectual property. If so, legal expertise should be retained to ensure that the intellectual property is protected and that appropriate agreements are in place with respect to authorized usage.

The board should consider other legal requirements and ensure that they are complied with by the organization. For example, the board may need to consider the legal authority for the organization to commercialize intellectual property, especially if doing so would jeopardize the charitable status of an organization. If the commercialization becomes, in effect, a business activity, it may be prohibited in the circumstances of a particular charitable organization.

C HUMAN RESOURCES

1. Introduction

Human resources are, for most organizations, a major "asset" in carrying out the activities of the organization and fulfilling its objects. Without humans, organizations could not make decisions, operate or meet their mandates. People are what charitable and not-for-profit organizations are about and what makes those organizations work. As with businesses, the product may be goods or services, but the strength of the organization comes from its people and people are most organizations' most important asset.

The human resource asset involves two major groups — employees and volunteers. Directors are, generally, volunteers in charitable and not-for-profit organizations and some of the comments in this chapter will apply to them as volunteers. However, they are unique volunteers in that they more than any other volunteer set the tone of the organization, make the decisions that should matter and plan for the future. They are more accountable than other volunteers or even employees.

This text is not intended to cover all human resource issues. There are a number of matters that are covered in other texts in this series. A board of directors should, from a human resources perspective, have in place a number of policies or measures to ensure compliance with legal obligations as an employer or as a good manager of the affairs of the organization. Directors of organizations that have employees ought to have in place updated policies and procedures on:

- hiring and retaining employees, including application forms that comply with the law and meet the needs of the organization;
- employment contracts or package of materials that includes job descriptions, reporting and lines of accountability, performance expectations and performance review cycles;
- maintenance and security of the personnel records that complies with the CSA Model Code;
- employment handbook or manual that sets out the relevant policies that operate in the workplace;

- training opportunities;
- discipline process that provides for graduated disciplinary measures reflecting seriousness of contravention and record of employee, application of process and fairness to the employee;
- occupational health and safety policies, including employer's duties, health and safety committees and employee refusal to do unsafe work.

If the workplace is unionized, there will be other matters with respect to labour relations that will also need to be addressed by the board of directors and senior management.

II. Selected Policies to Protect Human Resource Assets

a) Overview

There are some policy matters that go to overall management of human resources as an "asset", where the board wants to protect the value of this critical asset — workplace harassment and discrimination and conflict of interest. The policies are also central to the modern workplace, whether staffed with employees or volunteers. In addition, they are legal requirements on the board to ensure that there is compliance with the common law and statutory law with respect to human rights and workplace harassment and discrimination.

b) Workplace Harassment and Discrimination

Workplace harassment and discrimination has become a major issue in Canada for boards of directors. Aside from the serious consequences it can have on individuals, harassment and discrimination can poison the workplace for all employees and volunteers. It can, as a result, lead to a less efficient and effective organization — one that is not meeting its mandate. From a public perception perspective, of all entities, one would expect charitable and not-for-profit organizations not to permit or acquiesce in workplace harassment and discrimination.

A policy on workplace harassment and discrimination should include the following elements:

- Definitions

    - definition of harassment, one that incorporates discrimination based on a ground prohibited by the relevant human rights code, such as the Ontario *Human Rights Code*.[7] A typical definition of harassment involves a course of vexatious comment or conduct that is based on one or more of the prohibited grounds under human rights legislation with respect to another person. It would also establish the circumstances in which that course of comment or conduct is prohibited, e.g., where the person who engages in the conduct knows or ought reasonably to know that such comment or conduct is offensive to or considered unwelcome by the person to whom it is made. A policy could also refer to other persons who may hear the comment or see the conduct as part of the definition. Workplace harassment and discrimination can affect not only the "target" person but others, individuals who may be too shy or fearful to speak up against it.

- a definition of sexual harassment and discrimination. This definition could be incorporated into the broader definition of workplace harassment and discrimination, however, some policies will make a distinction between the two definitions given the nature of sexual harassment and discrimination. The definition should be gender neutral and recognize that the victim and the harasser could be male or female.

Sexual harassment and discrimination is generally where an individual receives unwelcome sexual attention from another person and such comment or conduct is known or should reasonably be known to be unwelcome. It would also include a situation where an individual is threatened or penalized by loss of job (including volunteer position), or advancement, or a raise or other benefit is denied for refusing to comply with any sexual demands by a person in position of authority who knows or should reasonably know that the sexual attention is unwelcome.

Sexual harassment and discrimination definitions will sometimes include a list of behaviours that are deemed to be inappropriate conduct. The list is intended to be illustrative and to cause people to reflect on their own conduct, and to allow for corrective action before the matter rises to the next level. The list could include any form of reprisal or threat of reprisal for rejection of a sexual solicitation or advance; unwanted touching,

---

7 R.S.O. 1990, c. H.19.

patting, pinching or other contact; physical assault; remarks that are suggestive or sexually aggressive; remarks, jokes and other comments that are sexual in nature; comments about physical appearance; leering; the display of pornographic pictures or sending of such pictures; sexual assault;

- racial or ethnic harassment and discrimination — some policies will also include a definition of racial or ethnic harassment and discrimination. It would include remarks, jokes or innuendo, the display or sending of racist, derogatory or offensive materials; insulting gestures or practical jokes based on racial or ethnic grounds.

There are some unique issues facing charitable and not-for-profit organizations. The high level of volunteers in the sector is a reality for many organizations. People volunteer for a variety of purposes — some purely altruistic, others to obtain the training required for employment and some for advancement in their own jobs. Whatever the reason behind the individual volunteering, he or she ought to be treated with the same level of respect as any other person in the workplace. Sexual harassment and discrimination (or workplace harassment and discrimination in general) is not any less unacceptable because the target is a volunteer as opposed to an employee.

The harassment and discrimination could also come from a customer, client or member, especially where the organization is involved in social services. The employee or volunteer will sometimes be alone and away from the place of business. Arguably, the policy should extend to include such situations. While the organization may not have the same internal mechanisms to address the harassment and discrimination (e.g., disciplinary action against the harasser), it may have others, such as suspension of privileges for the customer or member.

- Principles

The policy ought to focus on a couple of areas:

- prevention of harassment and discrimination;
- resolution of harassment and discrimination in a way that is least disruptive to ongoing working relationships;

- processes to be used are fair, responsive, timely, impartial and confidential. The procedures must be applied consistently and should attempt to preserve self-respect, dignity and the rights of all persons.

  Policies sometimes articulate a "zero tolerance" approach to harassment and discrimination. How realistic is a zero tolerance policy in any organization? Does it reflect how workplaces operate? Or is it a goal? Likely, as a matter of principle, it is an acceptable principle, but it is one against which the organization will be measured. A principle of zero tolerance may not always work and could result in a defensive stance by some individuals.

- Preventive Measures

It is generally less expensive and more effective to prevent problems than to clean up a problem. Any workplace harassment and discrimination policy ought to include measures, such as communication about the policy, that will prevent harassment and discrimination. The communications may prompt individuals to examine their own behaviour; at the very least, communication to employees and volunteers about the harassment and discrimination policy will put them on notice.

Employees and volunteers should be informed about the procedures to be used and their rights and responsibilities on those procedures. There should be a confidential process by which employees or volunteers could obtain advice and information or to report any incidents — whether against them or others. Confidentiality is important but employees and volunteers ought to understand that if the information is evidence of an offence, it could be reported to the police. To assist, the board should consider the appointment of a "workplace harassment and discrimination advisor" who is responsible for implementation of the policy and its procedures, provides advice to employees and volunteers, and training and other preventive measures.

The policy could also include information being given to the board of directors or the president as part of management's responsibility to report incidents to the board or the president. The information to be provided may differ depending upon the circumstances.

- Procedures

  Any policy should have procedures in place. It is one thing to say "we do not tolerate harassment and discrimination" but it is through procedures that harassment and discrimination is dealt with by an organization. The procedures should state who has responsibility to do what, including employees and management.

The employee's or volunteer's responsibilities include:

  - to inform the other individual that the remarks, conduct or behaviour is unwelcome and offensive. However, not all employees or volunteers will be in a position — or feel that they are in the position — to do so. If that is the case, they should seek the advice of the advisor;
  - to record as soon as practical the incident with as much detail as possible, including others present, where, time, and what specifically happened;
  - the procedures should recognize that the above two responsibilities will not always occur and that a complaint is not dependent on them. Rather, the procedures should indicate that detailed information is important to assess the situation, to resolve the complaint and to take appropriate preventive or disciplinary measures. If the evidence is weak or the complaint is dated, disciplinary measures against an employee or volunteer may not be justified;
  - a complaint ought to be brought to the attention of the appropriate person. Who the appropriate person is will differ from organization to organization. In some cases it may be the president; others, a senior manager. The key is to identify the person or position, who will then be responsible for the next steps.

- Management has several critical responsibilities:

  - the procedure should note that management is responsible for preventing and discouraging harassment and discrimination and that it is their duty to do so;
  - managers who are advised of a complaint shall take steps necessary to ensure that no reprisal or threat of reprisal is made

or taken against any person by reason of that person having made in good faith a complaint of harassment or discrimination;
- whether or not a complaint is made, management must take appropriate action in a timely manner when becoming aware of any possible violation of the policy;
- if there has been criminal behaviour or what appears to be criminal behaviour, it may be necessary to report the incident to the police.

- Reporting Procedure

The board should consider to whom a complaint is to be reported. In some cases, the board may want to be involved in the matter. Or it could delegate to senior management the responsibility for investigating (including by an independent, outside investigator) the complaint, the review of the report, the making of recommendations, the use of any alternative dispute resolution, and any disciplinary measures that ought to occur.

- Investigation of a Complaint

An allegation or complaint of harassment or discrimination ought to be kept confidential to the extent possible. However, usually a complaint or allegation cannot be investigated unless the person conducting the investigation interviews people, obtains legal advice and so forth. If any further action is required, it may be necessary to provide the information to other persons, such as police.

A complaint should be carried out by an appropriate and neutral party. Sometimes it may be necessary to retain somebody with experience outside the organization. The investigation should meet the minimum standards expected of any investigation, including separate interviews of the purported harasser and the complainant; interviews with witnesses; review of information; determination of whether or not there is sufficient evidence; and determination of whether or not there is a basis to resolve the complaint through mediation or otherwise.

A practice has developed in this area for the investigator to prepare a written report and provide a copy to the individuals concerned for comment on the accuracy and completeness of the draft report. The draft report should be kept confidential and the draft should be given only with the undertaking that it will not be given to anyone else except legal counsel or other representative or any person who accompanied the individual to any interview or meeting with respect to the matter.

- Confidentiality

  To the extent possible, all information should remain confidential and secure during the resolution of any violations. However, there are circumstances in which confidentiality cannot be assured. For example, if there is reasonable and probable grounds to believe that a criminal offence has occurred, the police ought to be notified. The board or management may want to consult with legal counsel to assist in making this assessment.

  Individuals who made statements should have access to those statements and the personal information contained in them. For example, the complainant, respondent and witnesses should have access to their own statements. The complainant and respondent should have access to sufficient information that they know what the allegations and responses are of the individuals involved, including witnesses, so that they can either defend themselves or rebut the information.

  Personal information may be very sensitive. It should be collected, used and disclosed only for purposes of the policy, dealing with a complaint, determining the appropriate means to address the complaint and to manage and resolve any contraventions, including disciplinary actions, remedial activities and other consistent or related purposes. It may be necessary, for example, to maintain certain personal information to monitor the employee or volunteer to ensure compliance with any resolution and to prevent future problems.

- Final Report

  The final report, including any conclusion, will be prepared by the investigator. It should be reviewed by the senior person responsible to determine, among other things, what measures could be put in place to prevent similar situations from occurring. The senior person could be management or the board. A copy of the report should be kept, but separate from the individuals' personnel files. The complainant ought to be informed about how the matter has been concluded if the complaint has been substantiated. The outcome, such as disciplinary action, should be recorded on the personnel file. If the investigation concludes that the complaint is not substantiated, no record of the complaint should be placed on the respondent's personnel file.

- Fear of Reprisal

  The policy ought to make clear that an employee or volunteer who makes a complaint should not fear reprisal or discipline or retaliation.

- Disciplinary Action

  The policy should outline the range of disciplinary action that could occur, which may include dismissal. The policy should allow for graduated penalties and for penalties that reflect the circumstances of each case. Even where there is a zero tolerance approach, there will be different graduations of harassment or discrimination, seriousness of the situation and impact on the complainant and the workplace.

- Malicious Complaints or Allegations

  A malicious or bad faith complaint is one that is made by an employee or volunteer who knows that the allegations are not true. Such complaints can legitimately be the basis for disciplinary action against the complainant. However, care needs to be taken in doing so. The policy should, at the very least, note that malicious or bad faith complaints are also a violation of the policy.

- Review of Decision

  Either the complainant or the respondent should have the ability to request a review of the investigation and the final report. To whom that review is addressed will depend upon who made the final decision. If the board made the final decision, it may be difficult for it to review its own decision, absent new evidence.

The Ontario Human Rights Commission and other human rights commissions will provide information about preventing harassment and discrimination in the workplace. The Ontario Human Rights Commission, for example, publishes a guide on hiring procedures that includes a model application form. *Hiring: A Human Rights Guide*[8] describes what is discrimination in employment and reviews advertising, application forms, employment interviews, and requesting a copy of the applicant's driving licence. It provides sample questions that may be asked and what may not be asked and deals with issues that are not always readily apparent. For example, a driver's licence will include information about the age of the applicant and may include information about disabilities.

The Commission also publishes materials about sexual harassment and other forms of harassment and suggestions on how to prevent it from occurring.[9] These suggestions include:

- developing an easy to understand policy and posting it in places where everyone can see it;
- using newsletters to make people aware of the policy;
- making information on the Commission available to employees (and volunteers);
- meeting with employees (and volunteers) to discuss the issue, how to prevent it and how to deal with it when it happens;
- working with union or employee associations (if any) to prevent harassment and discussing the policy with the union;
- send a strong message — and consistent one — that harassment and discrimination is not permitted and will not be tolerated;
- disciplining those who harass or discriminate against another person.

The success of any policy will depend upon the availability of resources to implement it. The board needs to ensure that appropriate resources are available — including training — for the policy to be effective in preventing harassment and discrimination and dealing with it when it does arise. The policy and its procedures need to be fair and work towards resolutions where possible. They also need to be seen to be fair in their operations.

---

8 Ontario Human Rights Commission, *Hiring: A Human Rights Guide* (Toronto: Queen's Printer, 1999), approved by the Commission on March 19, 1997.

9 See, for example, *Sexual Harassment and other Comments or Actions About a Person's Sex* (Toronto: Queen's Printer), approved by the Commission on November 27, 1996.

c) Conflict of Interest

A conflict of interest policy is another policy that goes to the integrity of the workplace and the human resource asset. The policy ought to make it clear that employees and volunteers have an obligation to avoid conflicts of interest — actual, potential and perceived. However, in reality, conflicts of interest will arise and to address that issue, employees and volunteers are obliged to inform the appropriate person about any actual, potential or perceived conflict of interest.

Clearly, there may be differences in what is or is not a conflict of interest and its materiality between employees and volunteers and senior management and staff. Conflicts arise out of the context in which the individual works and their other interests or activities in life. The policies may be very broad or detailed in approach. The detailed approach is sometimes more informative, but runs the risk of "but it was not included on the list, so thought I could do it." The broad approach may be too vague to be helpful to employees or volunteers to avoid or to recognize conflicts of interest.

A board may also take different approaches with respect to what is or is not deemed to be a conflict of interest. For example, many organizations have professional staff. Some organizations want to encourage their professional staff to participate in the activities of their profession; other organizations want to discourage such participation. The participation is discouraged by viewing as a conflict any meetings during regular working hours, or not permitting the staff member to use the organization's equipment (telephone, computer, photocopier) to participate. Some organizations will fall into a middle ground, e.g., reasonable use or attendance with permission of supervisor and in a manner that does not interfere with the workplace.

The policy should also provide for a positive requirement on the employee (or volunteer) to report any actual, potential or perceived conflict of interest. The person to whom the report is to be made is an issue for the board to consider. In some cases, it may be to the executive director, to a manager or to the board itself. There should also be a mechanism for management to bring a conflict of interest to the attention of the employee or volunteer.

The policy may be reactive or take the initiative. For example, the policy could set out what the ground rules are, what is considered a conflict of interest and the procedure to disclose. Another approach is for the policy to require all employees to complete a conflict of interest declaration form either upon being hired or a periodic basis, such as annually sign a certificate of compliance.

There are several areas of conflict of interest that should be considered from a "policy perspective", i.e., what the board would consider to be a conflict and how to address:

- outside employment — which may impinge on availability of the employee or quality of work done for the organization. In some cases, the work may be inconsistent with the beliefs and values of the organization or be with a "competitor";
- contracts with the organization or affiliated organizations;
- use of the equipment or facilities of the organization;
- activities during regular working hours for the employee or volunteer;
- participation in professional or other organizations in which others may consider the employee or volunteer to be representing the views or positions of the organization;
- acting against the interests of the organization through membership in another organization that is contrary to the organization.

These are only some examples of the types of conflicts of interest that can and do arise. The board will also need to consider how far removed the conflict needs to be in order to be material. For example, is it a conflict if the spouse of the employee has a contract with the organization? Is it relevant whether or not the spouses are separated but not divorced, or are still residing at the same address? Or if the contract is with the child of the spouse, who is not the child of the employee? Would it matter if the contract is for a small amount? Or that it had gone through a competitive process? Each organization may take a different view of these and other issues.

The policy should set out a procedure on how to deal with any conflict of interest report or allegation. It should include the following steps:

- report of conflict of interest, including sufficient information for a reasoned decision to be made to a designated and appropriate person or position;
- investigation by that person or by another delegated to carry out the investigation;
- meeting with the employee or volunteer to review the information and to seek any further clarification or explanation
- preparation of a draft report for comment as to accuracy and completeness by the employee or volunteer;
- opportunity to respond to conflict of interest finding;

- decision by an appropriate person (senior management or board) on the findings and on any action to be taken. Another option is for senior management to prepare a final report with recommendations for the board's review;
- notification to individual of what decision has been made, including whether or not a conflict of interest exists, what measures are to be taken by the employee or volunteer and what disciplinary action may be taken.

  The board may also want to consider whether or not the individual could be exempted from the policy and under what conditions. There may be a range of measures that can be taken. It may not always be reasonable, for example, to require immediate divestment of an investment or business interest if it would result in losses to the employee and the conflict can be managed on an interim basis. Care must be taken in not being unreasonable or unrealistic in designing any measures to address the conflict. The goal is to resolve the conflict to the satisfaction of the organization, not to "penalize" the employee or volunteer unless penalization is necessary on the facts. Penalization would be appropriate if, for example, the employee or volunteer had refused to comply with a previous ruling or its terms and conditions.

Conflicts of interest are serious and ought to be considered in a serious manner. However, they do arise and will arise in people's lives, especially if they are active.

D VOLUNTEER MANAGEMENT

Volunteers are the backbone of many organizations and without them, it would be very difficult if not impossible for organizations to fulfil their objects. Millions of Canadians volunteer each year for charitable and not-for-profit organizations, donating many millions of hours to the betterment of Canadian society. The importance of volunteers is often recognized but too seldom do organizations move to promote voluntarism. Volunteer Canada, as part of the International Year of the Volunteer, developed the *Canadian Code for Volunteer Involvement*[10] which sets out a proposed code for use by organizations. It recommends

---

[10] (Ottawa: Volunteer Canada, 2001).

that the code be adopted by organizations as an integral part of operational practice.

The code identifies several values, guiding principles and organizational standards for volunteer involvement. It does so in a broader context of the organization and asks questions that go to the fundamentals of any organization — why is it there and what is it trying to accomplish. The code recognizes that the board of directors, employees and volunteers each have a role to play in ensuring that volunteers are an active component — a valued human resource or asset for the organization.

The values are not surprising. Volunteers are generally seen to be vital to a just and democratic society, something the Panel on Accountability and Governance in the Voluntary Sector explicitly recognized in its final report.[11] Volunteers strengthen communities, but do so in a way that benefits both the volunteer and the organization. Volunteering is based on relationships; people want to connect to others and to do so in a manner that is respectful and done with integrity.

Organizations need to recognize that volunteers are vital. Organizations need to make commitments to the volunteers — a commitment that will bring about effective volunteer involvement. Volunteers also have rights to safety and a supportive environment with adequate resources and an appropriate infrastructure to provide that support. On the other hand, volunteers need to make a commitment to the organizations and to be accountable to it. They must act reasonably, responsibly and with integrity — especially when they are providing the goods or services to the community on behalf of the organization. They are often the primary contact people in the community have with the organization.

Organizations should develop and put in place organizational standards. These standards need the support of the board of directors and senior management — support that also recognizes the role of volunteers. Policies and procedures need to provide a supportive framework, one that both defines and supports the volunteers. There ought to be a marriage between the volunteer's capacities and the work that he or she does. The volunteer experience should be meaningful. And it takes a qualified person within the organization to be responsible for the program and to ensure that it meets the needs of the organization, those being served and the volunteers.

---

[11] *Building on Strength: Improving Governance and Accountability in Canada's Voluntary Sector*, (Final Report Ottawa: February 1999).

Resources need to be available for volunteer recruitment and screening. Any screening process ought to be applied consistently and fairly to all applicants to be volunteers. It should also identify those volunteers who have the skills or experience that is required or can be used by the organization — or those who can be trained. Training of volunteers is also essential, including orientation to the organization, its policies (such as those related to conflict of interest and workplace harassment). Volunteers, like any asset, will require care and attention, which can include ongoing training, supervision, performance appraisals and other forms of feedback. They should be welcomed into the organization and be treated with respect and as valuable assets. Their contributions should be recognized and applauded.

A number of issues should be considered as part of any operational standards for an organization. Does the organization provide adequate and appropriate facilities and equipment for volunteers? Are they repaid promptly for approved out-of-pocket expenses? Is there adequate insurance coverage? Will the organization pay for membership in relevant organizations or for training and development?

Do the policies and procedures in place reflect the needs and circumstances of volunteers? Or is there a need for volunteer-specific policies? Does the organization comply with its own policies and with the law with respect to discrimination and harassment? Are adequate records maintained on volunteers and their activities? Have policies and procedures been communicated to the volunteer? If not, how can they be expected to know what is expected of them?

The organization will also need to put in place mechanisms to ensure that volunteers are doing what they are supposed to do. The mechanisms could include random checks, ongoing performance appraisals and feedback, surveys of the clientele, training opportunities to address any deficiencies and so forth. Where there have been contraventions of policies or of the law, these matters need to be addressed sooner rather than later. The organization will still be accountable for the behaviour of the volunteer and may be liable for any injuries caused by the volunteer. It may be necessary to "discipline" volunteers as one would an employee; the liability runs with the activities, not with the character of the person. But it would be unfair to hold a volunteer accountable if nobody ever told him or her what was expected of them, what their role was, what to do and how to do it, or provided the training necessary for them to do it.

Organizations may also want to consider a periodic audit of volunteer management in the organization.[12] An audit would include several elements:

- planning and resources for the volunteer program;
- coordination of volunteers;
- volunteer job design and descriptions;
- recruitment processes;
- interviewing and screening;
- orientation;
- training;
- volunteer/employee relationships;
- supervision of volunteers;
- recognition of volunteers;
- recordkeeping and reporting on volunteers;
- evaluation of volunteers and the impact of their services;
- volunteer input.

The audit would allow the organization to identify strengths and weaknesses but also ensure that the volunteer program is meets the objectives of the organization. It can also lead to a more fundamental thinking about the organization and its programs — what is effective and efficient and what is not.

E INSURANCE AND INDEMNIFICATION

1. Directors and Officers

Insurance and indemnification are usually dealt with as methods of protecting officers and directors from liability. However, from another perspective, these practices can be seen as protecting the assets of the organization. Insurance and indemnification are flip sides of the same coin.

Indemnification in law is the saving of one person harmless or to secure against loss or damage.[13] Normally, when indemnification and directors and officers are discussed, the topic is indemnification of the directors and officers by the organization. To this end, incorporating legislation provides that the corporation may indemnify the directors.

---

[12] See S.K. Ellis, *Volunteer Management Audit* (United Way of America, 1992).

[13] *Black's Law Dictionary*, 4th ed. (St. Paul, Minn.: West Publishing Co., 1968) at 910.

Section 80 of the Ontario *Corporations Act*[14] and section 93 of the *Canada Corporations Act*[15] provide for similar authority to indemnify directors out of the assets of the incorporation.

The form of the indemnification is essentially the same in those two statutes and in similar statutes in other provinces. The officers and directors may be indemnified for all costs, charges and expenses that the director or officer sustains or incurs as a result of a lawsuit or other legal proceedings arising out of the execution of his or her duties of office. The wording of the typical section in a by-law for an Ontario-incorporated corporation reads:

> The corporation shall indemnify and save harmless the directors, their heirs, executors and administrators, and estates and effects, respectively from time to time and at all times from and against:
>
>> all costs, charges and expenses whatsoever that he or she sustains or incurs in or about any action, suit or proceeding that is brought, commenced or prosecuted against him or her, for or in respect of any act, deed, matter or thing whatsoever made, done or permitted by him or her in the execution of the duties of his or her office; and
>>
>> all other costs, charges and expenses that he or she sustains or incurs in or about or arising from or in relation to the affairs except costs, charges or expenses thereof as are occasioned by his or her own wilful neglect or default.

The standard by-law under the *Canada Corporations Act* is slightly different and reflects the statutory provisions under that legislation. But in principle, the by-law provisions are comparable.

The purchase of insurance — often called errors and omissions insurance or officers and directors insurance — is one method to provide such an indemnification. The assets of the organization may not be adequate to provide any realistic level of indemnification to the directors. Also, the tying up of the assets for that purpose would prohibit the assets from being used for the carrying out of the objects of the organization. If the building had to be sold to honour an indemnity to the directors, that asset would no longer be available to provide services.

This factor gives rise to a question, especially with respect to charitable organizations — Are those provisions legal? Some question has arisen in Ontario, at least, as to the legality of the indemnity provision for charitable corporations. The argument is that as the directors are trustees

---

14 R.S.O. 1990, c. C.38.

15 R.S.C. 1970, c. C-32.

or akin to trustees, the clause would improperly put at risk the trust assets for the benefit of the directors as directors. They, of course, cannot personally benefit and, so the argument goes, the charitable corporation ought not to indemnify them. This issue would not apply to not-for-profit corporations that are not charitable; however, if the argument is valid, it would apply to deeds of trust and the trustees who are appointed to manage the affairs of the trust and to incorporated associations that are charitable.

It is far from clear that the argument is correct. The statutes make explicit provision for the indemnities. Letters patent filed pursuant to Ontario legislation include provisions at odds with other Ontario legislation governing charitable corporations. These mandatory provisions, one would think, ought to have similarly excluded the indemnification authorization if that was the intention.

However, the Public Guardian and Trustee in Ontario has argued that the indemnification is a form of "remuneration" paid to the directors which the mandatory provisions prohibit. While this position might have some merit with respect to the purchase of insurance by the charitable organization (corporation, trust or unincorporated association), the strength of the argument is less obvious in an indemnification. There are, in addition, protections in the standard by-law that would avoid the assets being used to indemnify if the directors did not act in good faith.

In the Ontario context, this issue has been addressed in amendments to that province's *Charities Accounting Act*[16], which would appear to allow for the indemnification of directors. The regulations under that Act allow for the indemnification of directors and officers and the purchase of liability insurance by the charity.[17] The board must, however, consider a number of issues before it authorizes the indemnification and/or purchase of liability insurance. The board must consider:

- the degree of risk to which the executor, trustee, director or officer is or may be exposed;
- whether, in practice, the risk cannot be eliminated or significantly reduced by means other than the indemnity or insurance;
- whether the amount or cost of the insurance is reasonable in relation to the risk;

16 Section 5.1 to the *Charities Accounting Act* was enacted by the *Courts Improvement Act*, S.O. 1996, c. 25, subs. 2(2).

17 *Approved Acts of Executors and Trustees*: O. Reg. 04/01.

- whether the cost of the insurance is reasonable in relation to the revenue available to the executor or trustee;
- whether it advances the administration and management of the property to give the indemnity or purchase the insurance.

There are other conditions to the purchase of insurance or the payment of the indemnity. For example, subsection 2(6) prohibits the purchase of insurance if, at the time of the purchase, it unduly impairs the carrying out of the religious, educational, charitable or public purpose for which the executor or trustee holds the property. No indemnity shall be paid or insurance purchased if doing so would result in the amount of the debts and liabilities exceeding the value of the property or, if the executor or trustee is a corporation, render the corporation insolvent. The indemnity must also be paid or the insurance purchased from the property to which the personal liability relates and not from any other charitable property.

The sense of these conditions precedent and restrictions are far from clear. It is even less clear what happens to the indemnity or the insurance policy if, at some time in the future, the Public Guardian and Trustee or a court determines that the board did not adequately determine if in practice the risk could otherwise be eliminated or significantly reduced before approving the indemnity or purchase of insurance. Getting even muddier is the issue of the timing. Would insurance purchased prior to the promulgation of the regulation be valid? Would new by-laws be required? What happens to incidents that arise from the period before the regulation came into effect?

In other Canadian jurisdictions, where there is no equivalent body to the Public Guardian and Trustee overseeing charities, directors and staff still need to be wary of the ambiguities in the law detailed above. It is quite conceivable that they could see insurance or indemnification measures that they had in place challenged in an application or action brought to enforce their organization's charitable purposes. If successful, such a challenge could leave directors and the organization exposed to considerably increased liability.

Given the lack of clarity in the law, boards are well advised to obtain legal counsel and engage in thorough discussion of these issues with their insurer or broker before considering indemnification or insurance measures. There may be legal steps needed to bring the organization on-side. Certainly, the conditions precedent need to be addressed before any new by-law is put in place to indemnify the directors.

The issue of indemnification and insurance should be seen as one that is intended to protect the assets of the organization, whether that organization is charitable or not-for-profit. Many of the individuals who can provide the skills and expertise needed by organizations are those with a real and reasonable interest in protecting their personal assets. Also, it is not so much the payment of damages that gives rise to the issue but rather the retention of a lawyer and others to defend oneself. Legal fees, the hiring of experts and so forth can be expensive, an expense that the organization will need to bear in any event to some degree.

II. General Liability

Insurance also extends beyond the officers and directors. Insurance is an important part of any "asset protection" policy of a board. Insurance protects the assets in two ways — (i) should an event cause damage to the asset; (ii) should the organization be held liable for damages to another person. The board should, therefore, consider the following matters with respect to insurance:

- maintain historical record of insurance coverage:

    - type of insurance coverage, e.g., occurrence basis versus claims made. If the policy is an occurrence basis one, it is particularly important to keep records of the insurance policies to determine what the coverage was at the time of the occurrence and who the insurer was;
    - list of insurers and list of insurance brokerages used.

- annual report on existing coverage and recommendations from insurance broker. The broker is a professional who is there to provide advice to the organization. The insurance coverage should be reviewed at least annually to make sure that it is still appropriate or if additional (or less) coverage is required;
- review and upgrade property insurance. This review should determine if the policy provides replacement cost if that is needed, and whether or not the property coverage is adequate. There may be a need to upgrade the endorsements. For example, if the organization has started to serve liquor at its events, it should probably have an endorsement for that purpose, which may be less expensive than obtaining separate coverage for each event. There may be exclusions

to coverage that should be reviewed and eliminated or, to save costs, added where the risk is minimal;

- review general liability coverage:

  - ensure adequate to cover future claims;
  - need to provide written disclosure of all changes in material risks to the broker;
  - liability insurance will provide coverage for negligent actions but does not generally provide coverage for intentional acts, criminal acts, fines and penalties, punitive and exemplary damages, wrongful acts of directors and officers (e.g., discriminatory practices or breach of fiduciary duty), pollution and contamination or liability for contractual breaches;
  - specific areas of liability may also be considered during a review to ensure that coverage is part of the insurance policy. For example, does the policy cover sexual or workplace harassment? The review should examine the coverage from the perspective of the activities of the organization and its employees and volunteers and assess where the risks are and whether or not coverage is available and appropriate;
  - who is covered is another issue for review. A board would want to consider whether the directors and committee members who are not directors, the general membership of the organization, volunteers, spouses (who often are coerced into volunteering) and so forth are covered by the policy and under what circumstances. The geographic coverage may also be an issue, especially if the employees or volunteers travel outside of Ontario;
  - coverage for non-owned automobiles may be appropriate, in particular if volunteers or employees use their own or rental vehicles;
  - fiduciary liability coverage is available and may be appropriate for organizations at significant risk for decisions or actions taken with respect to fiduciary responsibilities (i.e., where the transaction has, or could be imputed to have, the character of a trust). The board should consider obtaining this type of insurance;
  - professional liability coverage for specialized services, including counselling services. If there any professionals who are employees or volunteers, consideration should be given to any insurance

coverage that is available through their professional or regulatory associations;
- are legal defence costs part of or in addition to the coverage limit?

- Officers and directors insurance has other considerations, which parallel those of the general policy:

    - is the coverage justifiable? This issue would arise with or without the list of considerations mandated by the Attorney General in Ontario for charitable organizations. It is difficult to justify $2,000 for insurance out of a budget of $5,000 whether or not the organization is a charitable organization;
    - is the coverage adequate and appropriate to the risk?
    - what areas might be excluded from coverage, such as criminal acts, fines and penalties, libel and slander, wrongful dismissal, personal injury including mental anguish and distress, pollution and contamination. Directors and officers ought to be reminded that insurance is not necessarily as comprehensive as they may think, and that it does not allow them to do things they otherwise ought not to do;
    - is coverage for the directors and officers or is it for corporate indemnification? The difference may matter to the directors and officers as to who is being insured and who has rights under the insurance policy;
    - are former officers and directors covered or only existing ones?
    - are there any limits to geographic area of coverage?
    - are legal defense costs part of or in addition to the coverage limit?
    - should the same insurer be used as for the general liability insurance? There may be advantages to using a different insurer. Also, some officers and directors may have independent access to insurance through their existing employment (if participation on the board is seen as part of their employment duties) or their professional association. Similarly, officers and directors may be able to obtain an endorsement for coverage under their homeowner's policy.

If the organization owns property there will be a number of other insurance issues that will arise. The organization may want to consider purchasing additional coverage to protect against pollution and contamination, either emanating from or migrating to their property.

F FISCAL MANAGEMENT

Fiscal management is the board's management of the financial affairs of the organization. It is primarily concerned with issues such as cashflow and ensuring that the cash is there when the invoices are due. There are, however, obvious connections to other management matters, including investment policy, program management and review and so forth. Fiscal management is critical to the short and long term success of the organization. If the cash is not there, the operations cease — no matter what the long term prospects may have been.

The board ought to be concerned about several factors in fiscal management. These include:

- the regular payment of salaries or wages, benefits and any deductions which are to be remitted to governments or for pension benefits. As discussed earlier, the directors have a high standard of care with respect to these matters and directors may be held personally liable under the relevant statutes should salaries or wages and remittances not be paid. It may be worthwhile to treat the remittances for income tax and other employment-related taxes and premiums (employment insurance and Canada Pension Plan) and benefits as "trust" funds and deposit them into a designated account for that purpose if there is any question of having the cash to make the remittances when due. The board may also want a regular statement from the executive director certifying on a monthly or quarterly basis that all taxes and remittances have been made and that all salaries, wages and benefits have been paid;
- is the organization operating a deficit and, if so, for how long? The source of the deficit needs to be determined. It could be as a result of previous deficits which were financed and the payments on the loans are causing the annual deficit. Or expenses may exceed the budget or revenues may be lower than what was budgeted. In some cases, it may simply be a cashflow issue — a grant or contractual payment has not arrived. Or the board may have approved a deficit for good, or bad, reasons. Or investments may not be doing as well as expected, or poor investments were made resulting in poor returns.

Boards need to take into account cashflow issues in preparing budgets and in managing the fiscal situation during the year. The audit committee or, if no audit committee, the board needs to monitor the cashflow on a regular or as-needed basis. Banking arrangements and lines of credit may be appropriate, especially if there are regular peaks and valleys in revenues or expenses. A strong working relationship that is open and honest with its financial institution will help an organization to manage these peaks and valleys through various loan arrangements.

If the source of the problem is expenses that are too high, the board needs to examine its options to reduce those expenses. It may mean cutting programs or putting off other expenditures until the cash is available. Or the board may need to identify new funding or revenue sources, taking care to ensure that they are within the law and within the mandate of the organization.

There are different ways to fund deficits. The board needs to review its incorporating statute, constating documents (such as its letters patent, trust deed or memorandum of association) and by-laws to determine what the organization may or may not do. Charitable organizations in Ontario are limited in their authority to borrow monies. Section 59 of the *Corporations Act* permits the corporation to borrow money, but a mandatory provision in the letters patent for charitable corporations limits borrowing for current operating expenses. The borrowing power of the charitable corporation is not limited if it borrows on the security of real or personal property.

There are a number of financing options, all of which should be considered with legal and accounting advice. The organization could mortgage its real property, issue promissory notes that are not secured, issue bonds and debentures that are secured or unsecured, establish longer payment periods with its creditors or borrow against its accounts receivable. If the organization intends to issue securities, such as bonds or debentures, it needs to ensure that it has the legal authority to do so and that it has complied with any relevant securities legislation.

No security should be issued by the organization without adequate legal advice. Even if the organization is exempt from the securities legislation in the province, the holder of the security will have common law and other rights to full and proper disclosure. The level of disclosure and how it is made is one that requires both expert legal and accounting advice. A full and frank assessment of the risk of an investment in a security is a significant part of disclosure. Individuals who lose their investment in a security issued by the organization may not be content with a simple "sorry". They may want to go after the directors who approved of the prospectus or disclosure document to recoup their losses.

The board should consider establishing a sinking fund to retire debt. The sinking fund approach allows for the orderly repayment of debt. The board could also consider allocating any operating surpluses to the repayment of debt or to bring the level of debt to a manageable level. Similarly, the organization may receive an unplanned-for donation, which could be used to repay debt. Of course, if the donation is for a specific purpose, the organization needs to honour the donor's intentions.

The board should also be vigilant in ensuring that no improper uses of funds occurs. Deficits and large debt place stress on people. Individuals may be more apt to use improper fundraising techniques, to use special trust funds for other purposes, or to divert remittances for a few months in order to manage the cash flow.

G PROGRAM REVIEW

Program review is an important part of the board's responsibilities. Program review is a periodic review of an organization's programs to determine if the program is achieving the desired outcomes. A program review may also assess whether or not it is doing so in the most effective and efficient manner. While a program may be achieving its stated outcomes, if it does so at a cost that is bankrupting the organization, it will be unsustainable and may be considered reckless by the directors.

Program review also helps to determine what "assets" the organization should have to carry out its activities. The review may identify assets that could be better used for other purposes or assets that are required to do the job better. If a charitable organization has real property, it needs to make sure that the property is being used for charitable purposes. In Ontario, a program review will assist the charitable organization to meet its obligations under the *Charities Accounting Act*.[18] In most cases,[19] a charitable organization is prohibited from owning real property as an investment, although it may divest itself of the investment within three years. If the property is not being used for the charitable purposes of that charitable organization, it will be considered to be an investment. The common law would also seem to support this position, in particular if the

---

18 Section 8, R.S.O. 1990, c. C.10.

19 But see *Centenary Hospital Assn., Re* (1989), 69 O.R. (2d) 1 (H.C.) and *Incorporated Synod of Diocese of Toronto v. H.E.C. Hotels Ltd.* (1987), 61 O.R. (2d) 737 (C.A.) for exceptions where the ongoing ownership of real property for investment purposes because of other statutory provisions.

charitable organization had significant investments in real property to the point at which it was no longer really a charitable organization devoting all of its assets to charitable activities but an investment company. The proceeds from the sale of any such property are to be used for the charitable purposes of the organization.

The Panel on Accountability and Governance in the Voluntary Sector[20] identified program outcomes as an important method to demonstrate that an organization is doing good in a good way. It suggested that organizations look to assessing results and impacts of programs as an accountability tool and a planning tool. It adopted the definition of outcomes as being benefits or changes for participants during or after their involvement in a program. This definition is dramatically different from the traditional approach to measuring success, for example, program outputs that measured the number of people who participated in or used the services.

Of course, the traditional method has its value, in particular in determining costs on a per-user basis. It also is more easily adapted by a wider range of organizations. Outcomes based assessment and how it is to be implemented is not always readily apparent. It may be easier to use in social services agencies (although there would be debates within that sector) than, say, for cultural agencies. How did a play change an audience? Is that measurable? Can the organization collect the information that it needs to measure the outcomes over a period of time? Can it do so while complying with privacy rights of its audience members?

These comments are not intended to be critical of outcomes based assessment but rather, to illustrate that any new method to measure success will have its difficulties in design and implementation. There are limitations to any measurement tool and a board must understand those limitations before it adopts one approach over another. Indeed, it may need to use more than one approach in order to obtain a true assessment of the program and its value to its members or to the broader community.

Whatever approach is used, boards will need to grapple with three tasks:

- identifying the goals for the program, whether outcomes based or more traditionally based. The goals need to be realistic and achievable. There is little point in having "prolonged world peace and happiness" as a goal under either the outcomes based or

---

[20] *Building on Strength: Improving Governance and Accountability in Canada's Voluntary Sector*, Final Report (Ottawa: February 1999).

traditional approach to measurement. That goal is unrealistic and certainly beyond the capacity of any single charitable or not-for-profit organization;

- identifying or developing how to measure progress. The goals are just that, goals; the issue is how far towards those goals an organization has come. The goals may, over time, also adjust either as they are achieved or it is recognized that the goal cannot be achieved or is not relevant to the organization. The measurement of progress will be dependent on the collection and analysis of data that is relevant to the organization and to its goals;
- disseminating the information to those within the organization and those outside who have an interest in the results. The information should also be used in the planning process, including making decisions of whether to continue with the program, maintain as is or adjust it, to change the goals or the resources allocated to the program.

In response to calls from the public and funders for greater accountability, Canadian charitable and not-for-profit organizations are in the process of seeking better and more consistent means to measure success. Organizations have an opportunity to advance this process through finding or creating appropriate tools to measure their own success in meaningful ways, and through cooperation with others in determining and promoting evaluation standards.

H INVESTMENT POLICY

1. Introduction

Organizations will have a number of reasons to invest whether they are charitable or not-for-profit in nature. Although charitable organizations may be more restricted in their investments, boards of both need to take due consideration in designing and implementing an investment policy and in monitoring its implementation and investments.

The first step in any investment policy is to determine what is to be invested or what are the investments. This step is not necessarily as easy as it sounds. What is an "investment"? Is it the temporary use of an asset, such as cash, for investment prior to it being used for its final purpose? Or is it a capital asset, such as real property, that is used for purposes of the organization? Or is it the use of assets in an endowment fund which is intended to generate revenue for the organization's operational expenses?

All of these three examples could be considered investments for either a charitable or not-for-profit organization. The intention here is to focus on the temporary or interim use of assets, in particular cash or cash equivalents, and endowment funds.

II. Investment of Charitable Property

Over the last several years, issues around investments have become particularly problematic, especially for charitable organizations and others holding charitable property. Because charitable property is "trust" property, the laws of trust apply to the property, both the common law and statutory law. Organizations may also hold charitable property in general or for special purposes. While it was long thought that charitable property held for special purposes was "special", recent case law has forced a reassessment of this view.[21]

It seems that many charitable organizations and their investment counsellors operated on the assumption that the organization could make its investments in a simple manner. For example, the board could authorize an investment company to decide on what investments were appropriate. Often, these investments included mutual funds, especially if the desire was to take advantage of a rising market for stocks or bonds. However, a series of cases in the 1990s proved that approach to be in error.[22]

The legal situation was not tenable. Boards of directors were obliged to make investment decisions but could not delegate that decision. But many boards did not have the expertise to do so or could not meet in time to take advantage of opportunities or to reduce risks of losses in existing investments. Although the boards could obtain expert advice, the decision on individual investments remained with them. But the boards could not invest in mutual funds, an increasingly important method of investing which had several advantages — spreading of risk, expertise in investment decisions, broad choice in the marketplace and so forth. An investment in a mutual fund was an improper delegation of the investment decision.

---

21 See *Christian Brothers of Ireland in Canada, Re* (2000), 47 O.R. (3d) 674 (C.A.). That case, arguably, has reserved centuries of charitable purpose trust law. See for a full discussion of this issue D. Stevens, "Exigibility of Special Purpose Charitable Trusts: The Christian Brothers Ontario Court of Appeal and British Columbia Supreme Court Decisions", in *Fundamental New Development in the Law of Charities in Canada* (Canadian Bar Association – Ontario, Continuing Legal Education, October 27, 2000).

22 *Haslam v. Haslam* (1994), 3 E.T.R. (2d) 206 (Ont. Gen. Div.).

The potential exposure to directors was substantial even where the directors would appear to have acted in good faith, carried out due diligence in selecting an investment firm, provided reasonable and reasoned parameters of investments to the firm and monitored specific investment decisions. Because the directors had improperly delegated the investment decision, in Ontario at least, they had breached their duties as trustees or persons akin to being a trustee under the *Trustee Act*[23] and at common law.

Legislative amendments were introduced in Ontario to manage this situation. The amendments permitted the board to adopt a more modern "portfolio model" of investing. This approach moves towards an overall process for assessing investments and away from the prudence of making a specific investment.

The amendments to the *Trustee Act* came into effect on July 1, 1999. The *Trustee Act* requires a board to establish an investment policy on the basis of the "prudent investor rule". The board must consider the following statutory criteria:

- general economic conditions;
- the possible effect of inflation or deflation;
- the expected tax consequences of investment decisions or strategies;
- the role that each investment or course of action plays within the overall trust portfolio;
- the expected total return from income and the appreciation of capital;
- the needs for liquidity, regularity of income and preservation or appreciation of capital;
- an asset's special relationship or special value, if any, to the purposes of the trust or to one or more of the beneficiaries.

The board must also consider the need for diversification in the investment. In doing so, it would look to the requirements of the trust and the general economic and investment market conditions. Obviously, the board may want expert advice and is authorized to obtain it and to rely upon it if a prudent investor would rely on the advice under comparable circumstances. Although this provision is helpful, it may leave some more sophisticated board members in a difficult position where they may have a higher standard of care than other directors.

---

[23] Sections 26 and 27, R.S.O. 1990, c. T.23.

There are some remaining fishhooks in the amendments. The list of criteria may be difficult to implement in reality. The list places a high premium on the ability of directors to understand the criteria and to work with them. Even sophisticated directors may have difficulty in understanding and applying the criteria. Second, there is no express authority for delegation of investment decisions, with the exception of mutual funds. However, what are "mutual funds"? Do they include "segregated funds", which is a similar product issued by the insurance industry? In some ways and in certain market conditions, segregated funds may be a better investment than mutual funds, assuming that segregated funds are not mutual funds.

III. General Considerations

The board of an Ontario charitable organization, in reviewing a draft investment policy needs to consider the criteria set out in the *Trustee Act*. Boards of charities in other jursidictions will be governed by their province's trust legislation, which may afford them less guidance than the Ontario provisions. Manitoba,[24] New Brunswick,[25] Newfoundland,[26] Nova Scotia,[27] and Prince Edward Island[28] have also taken a "prudent person" approach for investments, with Newfoundland's and PEI's statutory provisions being very similar to Ontario's. Under the Alberta *Trustee Act*[29] and in British Columbia,[30] trustees are provided a list of investments that are authorized for trust funds, generally conservative in nature including government bonds and debentures, stocks in approved corporations and so forth. Other types of investments may be made only pursuant to a court order.

But all boards — charitable and not-for-profit — should take into account overall strategic direction of the organization and the context in which that direction was developed and adopted by the board. It should take into account its overall financial situation. Does the organization have a debt load that is excessive? If so, the best use of any funds may be to reduce that debt load. However, the funds may be impressed with a special purpose trust, such as for endowment fund purposes or for the

---

[24] Sections 68 and 69, R.S.M. 1987, c. T160.

[25] Section 2, R.S.N.B. 1973, T-15, as amended by S.N.B. 2000, c. 29, s. 1.

[26] Section 3, R.S.N. 1990, T-10, as amended by S.N. 2000, c. 28, s. 1.

[27] Section 3, R.S.N.S. 1989, c. 479, as amended by S.N.S. 1994-5, c. 19, s. 1.

[28] Section 2, 3, 3.1 to 3.5, R.S.P.E.I. 1988, c. T-8, as amended by S.P.E.I. 1997, c. 51, s. 1.

[29] Section 5 and 7, R.S.A. 1980, c. T-10.

[30] Sections 15 nd 18, R.S.B.C. 1996, c. 464.

operations of a particular program. If so, the board may not be in a position to use those funds for debt reduction.

The board should look to its medium and longer term revenue position. What financial return will be needed from the investments to meet any cash flow shortfalls? Or is the investment intended to fund longer term program development? The board may want to include in its investment policy a discussion of how it intends to address any shortfalls through other mechanisms, such as greater fundraising activities or reduction in operating expenses. This type of information can be used both to guide investment decisions and to justify those decisions. The prudent investor rule focusses on the process used to make investment decisions and the investment policy ought to demonstrate clearly that the board was prudent, reasoned and reasonable in developing its investment policy, whether the organization is charitable or not-for-profit.

The board will probably want to identify its primary objectives from the investments so that they tee-up with the strategic plan of the organization. For example, if an important feature of the strategic plan is to build a new facility for the operations of the organization in five years, that factor may be critical to the types of investments that will be made under the investment policy. On the other hand, if the organization is investing surplus cash solely on a short term basis to generate some additional interest or other revenue, it may want to restrict investments to those that can be cashed in on short notice without penalty. The objectives of the investment policy need to be clearly articulated so that the investments can be related to the objectives.

The investments made under the policy ought to be monitored by a committee of the board or by the board itself. If the investments are not meeting the objectives, the board may need to address the issue.

IV. Ethical Investing

A board may also be faced with concerns about its investments. A number of organizations, because of their objects or the religious or ethical background to the organization, may prefer not to invest in certain types of investments. Or, it may articulate its desires in a more positive manner, i.e., to make investments in only certain types of investments that advance its objects or that are consistent with its objects. This investment approach is sometimes called "ethical investing". "Ethical procurement" is another aspect of the overall approach that is developing within the sector.

The law is not clear on the issue. Indeed, in the 1980s, the lack of clarity caused Ontario to enact the *South African Trust Investments Act*[31] which effectively relieved trustees, including directors of charitable organizations, from any liabilities for deciding not to make investments in South African investments or to dispose of any such investment.

Short of legislative enactment, there is no clear common law position on ethical investments. Manitoba has permitted trustees to consider non-financial criteria in making investments.[32] Arguably, the board could consider the objects in its letters patent or other constating documents to determine whether or not the investment was within or outside those objects. For example, a medical health charity could argue that investments in tobacco companies was *ultra vires* because it was using charitable assets for a purpose inconsistent with its objects, i.e., to advance the medical health of Canadians. Similarly, a religious charity could argue on the grounds of religious freedom that it ought not to take into account only financial criteria in making investment decisions.

There are significant legal issues with this approach. First, the board will also be judged on the same basis for other investments. If the board decided against investments in tobacco companies, why did it invest in liquor companies? Second, in Ontario, the charitable organization will still need to marry up its investment decisions against the criteria set out in the Ontario *Trustee Act*. The organization will need to be able to argue that any ethical investments fall within those explicit statutory criteria.

The board of directors may be able to bolster its argument (and at this time it would be only an argument) on the basis of consultation with its members and regulators, evidence that the ethical investments were not materially detrimental to the organization, evidence that donors would decide against donating to the organization because of such investments, evidence that the investment would be inconsistent with its objects or evidence that it is contrary to its strategic plans. Similarly, there may be evidence that the investment in a "non-ethical" product will damage the organization's reputation. And reputation is a critical intangible asset of most charitable organizations, without which they could not survive or prosper.

A factual basis must be in place to justify an investment policy based on ethical considerations. Any investment policy that is based on non-financial criteria will need to be very well thought out and only carried

---

31 R.S.O. 1990, c. S.16. The statute was repealed in 1997 by section 12 of the *Government Process Simplification Act (Ministry of the Attorney General)*, 1997, S.O. 1997, c. 23.

32 Section 79.1 of the *Trustee Act*, R.S.M. 1987, c. T160 as amended by S.M. 1995, c. 14, s. 3.

out with legal advice. But the final test is how well the investment does. If the investment has comparable returns to other investments that may be available to the charitable organization, there may be no losses on which to base an argument that there has been a breach of duty.

This argument would probably be stronger with respect to new investments as opposed to selling an existing investment. Any investor is faced with a vast number of options, even a charitable investor. It would likely be easier to demonstrate that a new investment meets the statutory and common law requirements. However, in selling an existing investment (especially if a loss would occur on the investment), it will be much more difficult to justify that sale than a decision not to purchase.

V. Commingling of Restricted Funds and Special Purpose Trusts

Charitable organizations may have a number of special purpose trusts that need to be managed or that are otherwise restricted. There is an argument that the "contributed property" (cash or other property) could only be invested on its own and not with other investments. This argument posed serious practical difficulties. Organizations would be required to invest separately the $5,000 fund for scholarships, the $500 donation for an endowment fund and so forth. The bookkeeping requirements alone could be depressing to any treasurer. Technically, the funds could not even be kept in the same bank account and each would need its own account, increasing banking and administrative costs for the charitable organization. In addition, the commingling of these types of funds permitted more prudent investments, which spread the risk and allowed for better returns.

In Ontario, a regulation under the *Charities Accounting Act* authorizes the combination of restricted or special purpose funds with other property received for another restricted or special purpose.[33] The regulation allows the organization to combine the property in one account or in an investment, but only if doing so advances the administration and management of each of the individual properties. All gains, losses, income and expenses must be allocated rateably on a fair and reasonable basis to the individual properties in accordance with generally accepted accounting principles.

---

[33] Section 3, *Approved Acts of Executors and Trustees:* O. Reg. 04/01.

The board must also ensure that the following records are maintained for each individual property, in addition to other record keeping requirements:

- the value of the individual property immediately before it becomes part of the combined property and the date on which it becomes part of the combined property;
- the value of any portion of the individual property that does not become part of the combined property;
- the source and the value of contributed property relating to an individual property and the date on which the contributed property is received;
- the value of the contributed property immediately before it becomes part of the combined property and the date on which it becomes part of the combined property;
- the amount of revenue received by the combined property that is allocated to the individual property and the date of each allocation;
- the amount of the expenses paid from the combined property that are allocated to the individual property and the date of each allocation;
- the value of all distributions from the combined property made for the purposes of the individual property and the purpose and date of each distribution.

The board must also maintain records on the combined property, which parallel the records for the individual property:

- the value of each individual property that becomes part of the combined property and the date on which it becomes part of the combined property;
- the value of the combined property that becomes part of the combined property, the date on which it becomes part of the combined property and details of the individual property to which the contributed property relates;
- the amount of revenue received by the combined property, the amount allocated to each individual property and the date of each allocation;
- the amount of the expenses paid from the combined property, the amount allocated to each individual property and the date of each allocation;

- the value of all distributions from the combined property made for the purpose of an individual property and the purpose and date of each distribution.

The regulation places a significant record keeping obligation on the organization, for which the board of directors is responsible. It is not clear whether or not the regulation has any retrospective effect. The regulation seems to be future oriented. What happens to the situation where the funds are already combined? Does the organization need to un-combine those funds? Recreate the records needed? Obtain a court order to remedy the apparent breach of fiduciary duties? As of the date of writing, these matters had not been litigated; accordingly an Ontario organization that has combined its contributed property may want to seek legal advice on this issue.

For charitable organizations in other jurisdictions, common law precludes commingling of assets. Absent legislation permitting such commingling, organizations and their directors may be held in breach of trust where this practice occurs.

Chapter 5

MANAGING THE ORGANIZATIONAL STRUCTURE

A INTRODUCTION

Boards of Directors should periodically undertake a holistic review of their organization's structure. A comprehensive review may also be triggered by the organization embarking on a new and significant activity or venture, when there are organizational or financial problems or issues, and when strategic alliances are proposed. The intention is to ensure that the assets of the organization, especially for charitable organizations, are being used in the most effective and efficient manner and that risks are managed in an appropriate manner. Appropriate structures can influence and even dictate the success of meeting organizational objectives.

An organizational structural review may be limited to the organization itself and how to achieve its objectives through better by-laws, amendments to the letters patent and similar changes. Typically, such an internal review involves consultation with the organization's various constituencies to ensure that the needs of different stakeholders are taken into account in putting in place the new or altered structure. The review could also involve a broader approach that relates the organization to others of like mind or interests in their community, across Canada or throughout the world. In this case, more weight may be given to administrative practices in parallel organizations than to internal organizational dynamics in determining what changes are to be made.

An organizational structure set out in a deed of trust will be difficult to alter unless the deed of trust permits amendments. Similarly, if an unincorporated association does not have an amendment clause, approval from all the members would normally be required because the relationship among the members is contractual in nature. If the organization is a corporation, the incorporating legislation provides for amendments to the letters patent, by-laws and for the dissolution of the corporation. Although the *Canada Corporations Act*[1] does not provide for amalgamations, other incorporating statutes do.

Amendments to the letters patent are made through supplementary letters patent. There is a process to obtain approval of the membership to the application for supplementary letters patent. The supplementary letters patent may deal with any matter that could be part of a letters patent, including extending, limiting or otherwise varying the objects of the organization, changing its name, varying any provision of the letters patent or prior supplementary letters patent, providing for any matter or thing in respect of which provision may be made in letters patent under the statute, and converting into a company or corporation with share capital.[2]

Organizational change may also be made through the by-laws. The legislation authorizes amendments to by-laws and the standard by-laws also provide for amendments. In the case of corporations incorporated under the federal legislation, the Minister's approval is required for any amendments to the by-laws. However, the standard by-laws for *Canada Corporations Act* corporations permit the directors to prescribe rules and regulations. Rules and regulations that are not inconsistent with the by-laws could be used for organizational matters.

Amendments to the letters patent or the by-laws, though, are not always necessary to manage the organizational structure of the organization. In many cases, all that is needed is the ongoing revision to the strategic plan or other plans of the organization. Organizational restructuring could be carried out, as is discussed below, using contractual arrangements with other organizations, bypassing the need for any more formal processes. The key to any organizational structure is to ensure that it meets the needs of the organization and allows for an efficient and effective use of the organization's assets. As any organization matures and as its environment changes, the board may want to reflect on what is the most appropriate way to fulfil the organization's objects.

The board will want to consider a number of factors for any organizational structure:

- what options exist that would improve the efficiency of the use of the assets;
- what options exist that would make the organization and its programs more effective in fulfilling its mandate;

---

1 R.S.C. 1970, c. C-32.

2 Section 131, *Corporations Act*, R.S.O. 1990, c. C.38.

- how best to protect the assets held by the organization, including its intangible assets such as goodwill and its reputation;
- how best to minimize risks, manage the risks and minimize liability;
- what opportunities exist for expansion;
- what opportunities exist to coordinate efforts and to cooperate with other organizations.

There may also be a dichotomy or balancing of "control" and who will have control over the assets and operations with "liabilities" and how to minimize existing or potential liabilities. This chapter will review several models for organizational structures, including for national structures, strategic alliances, parallel foundations and business activities.

B STRUCTURAL OPTIONS FOR NATIONAL ORGANIZATIONS

I. Introduction

Fundamental to establishing a multiple national structure is the concept that a not-for-profit organization does not permit equity ownership and therefore cannot be controlled through the usual means of share ownership.[3] With a profit-making share capital corporation, effective control can be maintained over a multiple corporate structure by the parent corporation owning a majority of the shares in subsidiary corporations. Variations on this relationship can involve a parent/subsidiary corporate model or a holding/operating company model. However, with a not-for-profit corporation, there are no shares that can be bought or sold and therefore no ability to control the corporation through the means of equity ownership.

Instead of having shareholders or owners, a not-for-profit corporation has only members, whether the corporation is incorporated at the federal level in accordance with the *Canada Corporations Act*[4] or at the provincial level in accordance with applicable provincial legislation, such as the Ontario *Corporations Act*.[5] However, corporate members are not the owners of the not-for-profit corporation or its assets. Instead, a not-for-profit corporation has no legal owner, equitable or otherwise, except it-

---

3 This portion of the chapter is based on a paper by T.S. Carter, "National and International Charitable Structures: Achieving Protection and Control" in *Fit to be Tithed 2* (Toronto: Law Society of Upper Canada, 1998). The materials were edited and reproduced with the permission of Mr. Carter.

4 R.S.C. 1970, c. C.32.

5 R.S.O. 1990, c. C.38.

self. It is its own self-contained legal person that cannot be bought or sold. However, since there is no ability to "own" a not-for-profit corporation in the normal meaning, it is essential that there be effective mechanisms implemented to control member organizations by establishing either integrated corporate structures or expedient contractual relationships.

The characteristic that is common to all national organizations is that their operations extend beyond the boundaries of only one province. It can do so through one of two options — on the basis of either a chapter model or an association model:

- Chapter Model
  The chapter model involves one legal entity acting as a single organization across Canada, normally involving multiple divisions at either the provincial level, the regional level, or at the local level. Those divisions are often referred to as chapters or branches. However, none of the chapters or branches are themselves separate legal entities. Instead the chapters or branches are a part of a single monolith legal entity. In some cases, such as registered Canadian amateur athletic associations, this approach may be required for income tax purposes.[6]

- Association Model
  The association model involves multiple legal entities, as opposed to only one corporation, that are organized at various levels, such as incorporated provincial associations or incorporated local organizations. The association model will have a governing body, normally established as a federal corporation, to act as the umbrella body over its member organizations, whether those members are corporations or unincorporated associations. An example would be local churches of a large national denomination. A member organization will normally have either a name or charitable purpose that is similar to that of the governing national association.

Although it is not difficult to draw a distinction in practice between the chapter model involving a single corporation and the association model involving multiple corporate entities, distinguishing between the two in practice is not always as easy. In fact, many national organizations currently operate without knowing whether they are a single corporation

---

6 See A.B. Drache, *Canadian Taxation of Charities and Donations* (Toronto: Carswell, 1996) at 10 to 12 for a discussion of this issue.

operating through local chapters or an association made up of separately incorporated members. A national organization that does not know whether it is organized as an association model or a chapter model will often perpetuate the confusion by encouraging local organizations to apply to become a chapter while at the same time creating a functional dichotomy by permitting or encouraging member organizations to be separately incorporated.

Even when it is clear that member organizations need to be separately incorporated as part of an association model, it may not be evident how those member organizations are to relate to the larger national structure. This is often the case with religious denominations that have seminaries, bible colleges, camps, or other related ministries that are expected to operate functionally "in sync" with the national denomination but without any corporate or contractual documentation in place to set out what that relationship is to consist of.

Significant problems can arise. For example, the board of directors of a member organization may strongly disagree with the direction being dictated by the national board. The national board may be surprised to find that it has no legal means to stop the board of directors of the renegade member organization from adopting a policy or course of action that was totally contrary to what was acceptable at the national level. When this happens, it will normally be too late to do anything about the lack of control over the renegade organization. The time to do something to avoid the loss of control is before the disputes arise with a member organization by developing and implementing an effective structural plan.

II. Pros and Cons of the Chapter and Association Models

a) Chapter Model

The most significant benefit of the chapter model is that by requiring only one corporation, it is much easier to maintain a higher degree of control over chapters or branches without the necessity of contract or licence agreements that are otherwise required with the association model. In addition, by utilizing only one corporation to carry on operations on a national basis, there is generally more symmetry and coherency over day-to-day operations and control of personnel.

A chapter model also does not run the risk of losing its assets, goodwill, donor base, or trade-marks to a "renegade" member organization, since legally everything is owned by the single national corporation. A chapter or branch would have no legal right to take any assets on its own if it was to leave the national organization.

The most fundamental problem inherent in the chapter model is that by having only one corporation, the liabilities that occur in the operations of one chapter will expose all of the assets of the national organization to claims arising out of activities of that one chapter even though other chapters may have had nothing to do with the incident in question. Similarly, even if the incident involves a national program involving all chapters, there is no ability to protect specific assets of the national organization, since all assets are owned by the national organization.

Even if the national organization was to set up individual charitable trusts to fund specific programs, the assets contained in those charitable trusts could still be subject to claims by those who were able to establish a causal connection between the trust fund and the incident that allegedly led to the injury or abuse that they had suffered.[7] Given the increased exposure to liability faced by charities arising out of claims associated with sexual abuse, every national organization that is currently organized on a chapter model should carefully review whether or not it can afford, from a risk management context, to remain as a single legal entity. For national charitable organizations that have programs involving low exposure to liability there will understandably be less reason to change from a chapter model structure.

b) Association Model

There are a number of advantages in utilizing the association model over that of the chapter model. The primary benefit is that of reduced liability exposure for the organization by containing the liability attributable to each member organization within a separate corporate entity so that the claims made against a member organization do not affect the assets of other member organizations or that of the governing body. In the event that one member organization owns real estate that is subject to toxic contamination, the cost associated with the cleanup of the contamination will generally be limited to the incorporated member organization as opposed to affecting the assets of other member organizations or of the governing body of the national association.

---

7 The Ontario Court of Appeal decision in *Christian Brothers of Ireland in Canada, Re* (2000), 47 O.R. (3d) 674, may have extended the potential liability by eliminating even the need for a causal connection. However, the full impact of this decision is difficult to discern and, arguably, it may be limited to situations in which the corporation is being wound-up due to insolvency. Further case law will be necessary to determine how far the Court of Appeal's decision goes.

If a member charitable organization was to become involved in activities that result in its deregistration as a registered charity with Canada Customs and Revenue Agency, only the charitable status of that member organization would be at risk instead of the charitable status of other member organizations or the national association itself. For national charitable organizations that carry on operations in Ontario, the creation of a separate charitable corporation in Ontario to oversee Ontario activities would mean that the jurisdiction of the Public Guardian and Trustee in Ontario would generally be limited to only the assets of the Ontario charitable organization instead of affecting those of the national association or member organizations in other provinces.

Another benefit of establishing a separate corporation in Ontario is that the operations of the national organization that are carried on outside the province of Ontario through separate corporations in other provinces would not be subject to the provisions of the *Charities Accounting Act*.[8] Subsection 6(8), for example, permits an individual to apply for an *ex parte* order to require a public inquiry by the Office of the Public Guardian and Trustees in the event of complaints concerning the solicitation of funds and the manner in which those funds are utilized. Similarly, a national organization may be able to avoid the investment power provisions in the *Trustee Act*.[9]

The jurisdiction of the Ontario Public Guardian and Trustee over non-Ontario charitable organizations is not entirely clear. If a charitable organization based in Alberta fundraises in Ontario, its activities in Ontario are probably covered. However, to what extent may the Ontario Public Guardian and Trustee demand information and books and records with respect to activities outside of Ontario? Would it matter if the funds raised in Ontario are directly traceable to those activities? Could an order of the Ontario court be readily enforced against the Alberta organization in Alberta? Or another province?

National organizations face similar issues. If the charitable organization is based in Ontario but operates throughout Canada, there is a stronger argument that the Ontario Public Guardian and Trustee has jurisdiction over all of its activities — in Ontario and outside of Ontario. This position is not certain, but there is a strong argument in favour.

The courts and regulators will look to the operations of the organization and what its intentions were. Where is the head office? Where are its employees? Where are the books and records kept? Where are deci-

---

8 R.S.O. 1990, c. C.10.

9 R.S.O. 1990, c. T.23, as amended. The investment powers are discussed in Chapter 4.

sions made? These questions and other similar questions are not easily answered. Much will turn on the specific facts. However, if there is fraud or similar malfeasance involved in the activities, there would certainly be an incentive for other law enforcement agencies and for the courts to assist in correcting the perceived problems.

There are several disadvantages with the association model. The most obvious problem is that a governing body can easily lose control over its separately incorporated member organizations if appropriate steps are not implemented to ensure that the member organizations are subject to appropriate contractual and/or licensing control mechanisms. Often a member organization will need to utilize the name or trade-marks of the national association. However, if the name and/or logos of the national association have not been protected by obtaining trade-mark registration, or the usage of the trade-marks by member organizations is not properly documented through trade-mark licence agreements, then the ability of the national organization to protect and enforce its trade-mark rights may be seriously prejudiced due to unintentional infringement of trade-marks by member organizations as well as others.

If the member organizations have names that are similar to that of their national associations, there is frequently confusion that occurs in gifts given to the wrong charitable organization, particularly where testamentary gifts fail to properly describe whether the national association or the member organization is the intended beneficiary. This confusion could result in the estate having to apply for a *cy-pres* court application to determine which charitable organization is legally entitled to the testamentary gift.

Effective utilization of the association model requires the creation of multiple corporations and the implementation of numerous and sometimes complex control provisions. The complexity in the relationship could result in serious confusion unless the control mechanisms are carefully crafted and consistently applied. Failure to take appropriate steps in this regard could result in a state of confusion that might be even more problematic than the liability risks associated with the chapter model.

III. Association Model

a) General Considerations

The board will want to take into account several legal factors before making a decision on which model to adopt. These factors include:

- federal versus provincial incorporation. Federal incorporation avoids the need for prior written approval of the Public Guardian and Trustee in Ontario. It also provides greater flexibility with respect to who may be a director and number of directors, and in the by-laws and in how the structure is implemented;
- letters patent, for charitable organizations, would need to have charitable objects that are national in scope to avoid acting *ultra vires*. The letters patent should also include an ability to establish and enforce standards and to coordinate and facilitate operations and, for religious organizations, to require directors to subscribe to the faith or doctrinal statement of the organization. The letters patent may also include broader investment powers, including those related to ethical investments. The dissolution clause should provide the assets on winding up being distributed to a charitable organization at the national level with similar objects;
- by-law considerations, including classes of membership, the structure of membership, voting rights, individual and organizational membership, nomination or election of representative directors and similar issues.

b) Control Considerations for the Association Model

Since each member organization within a national association will be a separate legal entity, it is essential that the matter of control over those member organizations be carefully addressed and that it be done in the early planning stages in the creation of a national association or during restructuring. Once member organizations have been created and are operational, it is generally very difficult for the national association to "rewrite the rules" and require that member organizations relinquish some measure of control back to the governing body. The national governing association will have little ability to exercise control over member organizations unless those organizations have agreed to operate under the control of the governing association by either amending the internal corporate documents of the member organization or entering into appropriate contractual or licence arrangements.

A frequently used method of indirectly controlling member organizations is through *ex officio* directors. The by-laws of the member organization would provide for *ex officio* directors who are either directors of the national governing board, or alternatively, hold officer positions in the national governing board created for the specific purpose of allowing those individuals to become qualified to sit as national representatives on the board of the member organization. Although the utilization of *ex officio* directors is an effective means of maintaining control, it should not be relied upon as the only means of doing so. It does not encompass contractual relationships that can articulate the expectations between a governing association and its member organizations or licensing considerations involving intellectual property. Furthermore, as discussed in Chapter 3, *ex officio* directors will owe a duty to act in the best interests of the corporation to which they are directors, which may create conflicts with their duties to the national organization.

A second approach is the "franchise" model. A parallel can be drawn between the relationship of a franchisor and its franchisees and the relationship between a national governing association and its member organizations. Just as a national governing association cannot control member organizations by owning the "shares" or other equity interest of a member organization, a franchisor, in a business context, is not the owner of shares in the franchisee corporation. As such, the franchisor must establish an alternative means of control over the franchisee. This is done through the contractual relationship of a franchise agreement.

The governing body of the national association can establish an effective contractual relationship between the governing association and its member organizations involving key factors, such as what are the requirements of membership in the association and the consequences of losing that membership. It can authorize the licensing of trade-marks and copyrights of the national organization. *Ex officio* directors and a franchise approach can be used to complement each other or be used independently, depending upon the circumstances.

The basic components involve:

- an effective association agreement;
- the inclusion of appropriate control provisions within the incorporating documents of member organizations; and
- the implementation of a licensing arrangement to deal with intellectual property.

The ability to enforce the various agreements and arrangements is central to this approach. Unless they can be enforced effectively and in a timely manner, they will not yield the necessary control over critical matters.

c) Decentralization through the Association Model

A national organization that is currently structured as a single legal entity based on the chapter model may at some point in the future decide to convert its operating structure to that of the association model.

Restructuring through decentralization — i.e., devolving elements of the operations or mandate of a national organization to multiple separately incorporated member organizations — is complicated by numerous legal factors. These include the following:

- if the member organization is to receive a transfer of assets from the national governing association, then those assets need to be set out in a bill of sale or other form of transfer agreement. In the case of a charitable organization, a transfer to a member organization presupposes that the member organization is already registered as a charitable organization, either because it previously obtained charitable status as an "associate" of the parent charity, or had applied for and received separate charitable status when the member organization initially became incorporated;
- if the property being transferred consists of real property, then a title search will need to be completed to determine if there are any restrictive trusts attached to the deed for the property being purchased that need to be complied with as part of the transfer. Restrictions in this regard could include a requirement that the church property only be used in accordance with a particular statement of faith or religious practice. If there are restrictive trusts, then the transferee organization, such as a local church, would need at the very least to agree in writing to comply with the terms of the restricted trust set out in the title documentation for the property;
- when donor-restricted trust funds are being transferred, such as when an estate endowment fund states that it is to be used for a particular local purpose, the investment powers that it apply to those funds will need to be identified and complied with by the transferee member organization. In addition, the transfer of donor-restricted special-purpose trust funds will generally require court authorization for a change of trustees or in accordance, in Ontario, with the *Charities Accounting Act*;[10]
- if the transfer of assets involves real property that may be subject to toxic contamination, as may occur from a leaking underground oil

[10] R.S.O. 1990, c. C.10.

tank, the transfer of real property should not take place until an environmental audit has been conducted and the directors of the transferee member organization have acknowledged in writing that they understand their potential exposure to personal liability arising out of the transfer of the property in the event that the property is subsequently found to contain contaminated materials;

- if the transfer of real property to a member organization is to be subject to a reversionary interest in favour of the national governing association, then the deed to the member organization would need to include an appropriate provision to establish a reversionary interest;
- if there are liabilities that the transferee member organization is to assume as part payment for the assets being received, such as the assumption of an outstanding mortgage, or unsecured debts, such as bonds or promissory notes, then there should be a clear description of what those liabilities are together with the consent of the creditors or secured party, if necessary.

d) Piercing the Corporate Veil

A fundamental reason for the association model is to limit liability within a single corporate entity. While the concept of limited liability protection is still the general rule for corporate entities, whether the corporation is in the form of a share capital or a corporation without share capital, there are a few instances where the governing body of a national association might be found to be liable for the actions of a member organization.

The law is not very clear on when the court will "pierce the corporate veil". In *Transamerica Life Insurance Company of Canada v. Canada Life Assurance Company*,[11] the court held that it is difficult to define precisely when the corporate veil can be lifted but that the lack of a precise test does not mean that a court is free to act as it pleases on some loosely defined "just and equitable" standard. The court went on to state in that case that the separate legal personality of a corporate entity will only be discarded when it is completely dominated and controlled and being used for fraudulent or improper conduct. "Complete control" involves more than ownership. It must be shown that there is complete domination and that the subsidiary company does not in fact function independently of the other corporation.

Although the context of this case was a business corporation one, it does provide some guidance for an association model approach. The

11 (1996), 28 O.R. (3d) 423.

board of directors of both the national governing association and the member organization should avoid circumstances that might lead to allegations of complete domination and control by the governing association over the operations of the member organization. Some of the factors suggesting "central control"are:

- common bank accounts or investments shared between the national governing association and the member organization;
- explicit or implicit representation that the national governing association is responsible for the operations of the member organization;
- both organizations occupying the same location for either operational or administrative activities;
- using the same officers or employees unless there is documentary evidence establishing that one organization is invoicing the other organization for the services provided by the employees of the other organization;
- having either the national governing association or member organization use the land, buildings or property of the other organization;
- having the executive director of the member organization act on the direction and in the interest of the national governing association;
- failing to observe the legal formal requirements of the member organization in its operations and direction;
- having the same individuals serving on the board of directors or key committees of both the national governing association and member organization;
- indicating directly or indirectly on letterhead, signs, brochures or other documentation that the member organization is an operating division of the national governing association;
- having the governing body pay the salary and other expenses or losses of the member organization;
- having the national governing association and member organization use the same lawyers or accountants on a regular basis;
- failing to have loans from the national governing association to the member organization properly documented and formalized through proper corporate formalities and authorization by board resolutions.

This list of factors is not intended to suggest that there cannot be some similarity in operations or some overlapping in control between a national governing association and a member organization. However, it is essential that the board members and key executive officers of both the national governing association and the member organizations understand that both organizations must operate as separate and distinct charitable corporations and as such must respect the autonomy and internal integrity of each organization.

IV. Chapter Model

a) General Considerations

Many of the comments described above concerning the internal structure of the association model have equal application to the structuring of an organization based upon the chapter model. The basic structural difference between the association model and the chapter model is that with the chapter model, the national organization is not only the governing body for the organization but is also the only legal entity through which the organization carries on operations throughout Canada.

The board will want to consider the following factors:

- federal versus provincial incorporation. Since a national organization based upon the chapter model will need to operate as a single legal entity in more than one province, it would be prudent for a national organization to be incorporated under the *Canada Corporations Act*. There are serious legal issues in converting from provincial to federal incorporation — a process that cannot be done directly but only through carefully planned and implemented machinations, especially for charitable organizations;
- letters patent considerations — the considerations set out above for the association model also apply to letters patent for the chapter model. The charitable objects contained in the letters patent or supplementary letters patent for a national organization based on a chapter model need to identify that the work of the charity can be carried out through divisions, i.e., chapters or branches. The objects of the national organization need to be broad enough to include not only the activities of the head office but also the activities that are carried out at the chapter or branch level to avoid an *ultra vires* issue;
- the by-laws need to address accountability issues, including those related to financial statements, policy statements and budgets. In addition, issues with respect to membership classes, nomination and election of directors and other representation of the chapters should be considered. The federal legislation and its model by-laws are flexible in this regard.

V. Chapter Agreements

When a chapter or branch is established, it operates as a division of the national organization instead of having created a new legal entity. However, often the members of the local chapter or branch do not understand that their establishment is simply an extension of the national organization and the branch or chapter does not have a separate existence outside of the national organization.

To clarify the relationship and to provide certainty concerning the establishment, operations and expectations of a chapter or branch, it is important that the national organization ensure that an appropriate agreement, usually referred to as a chapter or charter agreement, is in place when the chapter or branch is established. Some of the key considerations that should be part of a chapter agreement would include the following:

- recognition that the chapter or branch is an operating division of the national organization as opposed to being a separate legal entity on its own. As such, the continued existence of the chapter or branch will be at the discretion of the board of the national organization and dependent upon the branch or chapter complying with the chapter agreement;
- recognition that the organizational structure for the chapter or branch is to be reflected in the general operating by-law of the national organization;
- an explanation of the expectations of a branch or chapter, including those related to copyright and trade-mark usage, the minimization of risk and adherence to the policies and procedures put in place by the board of directors at the national level;
- an explanation of the circumstances under which the corporate name, trade-marks and logos of the national organization can be utilized by the chapter or branch;
- a statement that all donations and income received by the chapter or branch are the property of the national organization and under its control and are therefore to be accounted for in the consolidated financial statements for the national organization. The required financial accountability will necessitate that regular reports by chapters or branches be given to the national organization, preferably on a monthly basis, or as frequently as is necessary in the circumstances. There may be issues with respect to the use of any charitable gaming proceeds and the books and records for a lottery

scheme conducted and managed by the branch or chapter. Typically, those must remain within the province that issued the licence;

- an explanation of the circumstances under which the grant of a charter will be terminated and the consequences that will flow from such termination. Some of those consequences would include the chapter or branch turning over all of "its" property to the national organization, ceasing to carry on operations and agreeing not to use the corporate name, logos and other trade-marks of the national organization. In addition, the chapter or branch would be required to return all donor lists and agree not to contact any donors in the future;
- in the event that a chapter or branch obtains its own charitable registration number with Canada Customs and Revenue Agency, it would be required to apply for "associate" status to allow for a transfer of funds between the chapter or branch and the national organization in excess of the normal 50% maximum of receipted donations for the previous year. The local chapter or branch should be required to submit its application for charitable registration to the national organization for approval before it is made to the Canada Customs and Revenue Agency;
- identify whether the chapter or the national office is to obtain general liability insurance for the operations of the chapter. Normally this should be done by the national office, since the national organization is the insured legal entity. It is important to ensure that the name of the national organization as well as all related chapters or branches are shown on the general liability insurance policy. Further, if directors and officers liability insurance is obtained, then the names of the members of the controlling board for each local chapter or branch should be shown on the policy in addition to the names of the directors of the national organization.

C PARALLEL FOUNDATIONS

Parallel foundations are public foundations that are established by a charitable organization.[12] The charitable organization is intended to carry out the charitable activities and the parallel foundation raises funds to assist that charitable organization to do so. The foundation may also

---

12 See R. Jane Burke-Robertson, "Establishing a Parallel Foundation: Why (or Why Not) and How", in *Fit to be Tithed: Risks and Rewards for Charities and Churches* (Toronto: Law Society of Upper Canada, Continuing Legal Education, 1994).

carry out charitable activities on its own, which may or may not be broader than those of the charitable organization. The parallel foundation is registered as a charity pursuant to paragraph 149.1(1)(a) of the *Income Tax Act.*[13]

Under that Act, the foundation must be either a corporation or a trust and must be created and reside in Canada to comply with the statute. The majority of its directors or trustees must, therefore, be residents of Canada. More than 50% of the directors, trustees, officers or officials must deal with each other at arm's length and not more than 50% of the contributed capital can come from one person or group of persons not dealing at arm's length. If not, the foundation will be a private foundation.

There are a number of reasons to establish a parallel foundation.

- establish an endowment fund — Because it is a foundation, it can create an endowment fund for the benefit of the charitable organization more readily and easily than can the organization itself. The foundation can produce a regular source of revenue for the organization or for special projects that require longer term development. There are disbursement quotas for public foundations, but compliance with those quotas can still be accomplished while meeting this objective.
- segregating funds — The board may want to do so for several reasons, including minimizing the risks of those funds being claimed to pay for any liabilities (although issues around the *Bankruptcy and Insolvency Act*[14] need to be addressed if there is a transfer from the organization to the foundation and the organization was or becomes insolvent), distinguishing to donors between fundraising for operational purposes and for capital purposes, protecting surplus funds from future decisions by boards of directors or reducing surplus funds so that the organization becomes eligible for other funding or granting programs.

Parallel foundations are not for all organizations. They are more appropriate if the organization has received or anticipates receiving larger donations or bequests that are surplus to the current requirements. Similarly, if the organization has or is setting up a planned giving program, the foundation could be the target for those funds. However,

---

13 R.S.C. 1985 (5th Supp.), c. 1.
14 R.S.C. 1985, c. B-3, as amended.

the parallel foundation approach is probably not worthwhile for smaller organizations given the expenses involved in establishing and operating the foundation.

The board, if it decides to do so, should consider a number of issues. For example, will it be a trust or corporation? Will the beneficiaries be limited to the "parent" organization or broader? There is an argument that the beneficiary should not be limited to the parent organization but also permit the foundation to carry out charitable activities or provide funding to other complementary charitable organizations.

How should the organization be controlled? Given that at least 50% of the trustees or directors must be at arm's length from each other, there is a legal issue of who from the "parent" organization is on the board of the foundation. Also, if the relationship and control is too strong, it may be possible to pierce the corporate veil should the "parent" organization run into difficulty. The factors discussed above with respect to national structures are equally applicable to parallel foundations. In addition, the foundation may want to avoid allegations or actual conflicts of interest by having an independent committee make recommendations on grants.

If a decision is taken to establish a parallel foundation, the board of directors of the parent organization should be aware, and take steps to address, any administrative issues that may arise. Exclusive charitability (i.e, devotion of all an organization's resources to charitable purposes), subject to certain exemptions or exclusions set out in the legislation or at common law, is a requirement for qualification as a registered charity under the *Income Tax Act*. Sometimes a foundation is established by a not-for-profit organization whose objects preclude it from qualifying for charitable registration under the *Income Tax Act*, so it can carry on activities — for example, educational work — that qualifies as charitable. In these circumstances, the board of directors should take care to ensure the strict limitation of the foundation to its mandated activities and in particular take measures to prevent commingling of foundation funds with those of the organization. Failing to do so may jeopardize the foundation's charitable status.

Whether the parallel foundation is related to another charity or a not-for-profit, the board should anticipate likely confusion among donors between the two organizations. Directors should be cognizant of the need for having administrative measures in place to ensure against improper transfer of donations, particular legacies or endowments, between the two organizations.

D STRATEGIC ALLIANCES

Strategic alliances are commonplace in the commercial sector. The purpose of a strategic alliance is to permit two or more organizations, usually with a common or complementary interest or assets, to work together to achieve a specific result. A deciding factor to enter into a strategic alliance is whether or not the organizations will be able to achieve the common or complementary purpose more efficiently and more effectively than they could apart from each other.

There are a variety of strategic alliances, some of which are more formal than others. The boards of directors in assessing the value of a strategic alliance may want to consider the range of options that are available. Each of them will have their own legal and practical issues that will need to be resolved. In some cases, the toughest issues will be related to the emotional ties people have to a particular asset or program or to the "independence" of an organization, an independence that was maintained through the hard work and diligence of its members. A clash of "corporate cultures" may also be another constraint on the success of a more integrative strategic alliance.

The range of strategic alliances include:

- advisory committees to assist in the delivery of programs by one or the other organization in a strategic alliance;
- committee that would develop joint recommendations for programs, including budget, annual plans and so forth;
- contractual relationship between two or more organizations for the delivery of services by one organization to the others, such as administrative services;
- "joint venture" in which the organizations have a share or interest in the asset, such as a building that is used by several organizations;
- "joint venture" in which each organization will contribute to and participate in a project;[15]
- separate legal entity, such as another corporation without share capital, or business corporation that operates certain programs for several organizations, such as an office building;
- establishment of another corporation without share capital to operate programs on behalf of two or more organizations. Each of the

---

15 See discussion below on joint ventures outside of Canada under Foreign Activities. The same type of documentation will be required to demonstrate that the charitable organizations are each carrying out their own charitable activities through the joint venture.

organizations would enter into an agency or contractual arrangement by which the new corporation would deliver the charitable services, but it would do so in a more collaborative manner than would otherwise be possible;

- merger or amalgamation of two or more organizations.

There are several issues for a board to consider before it embarks on any of these paths. First, does the board have the political support to do so? In other words, does it have any mandate from its members and other stakeholders? This mandate will commonly not be there explicitly but the board needs to be sufficiently comfortable that it will obtain approval before proceeding too far down that road. There may also be obstacles at the staff level towards any form of strategic alliance. If the organizations have been historically in competition with each other, have different styles, or have little in common, there may be significant cultural issues to address, especially where the strategic alliance is further along the spectrum towards merger.

Second, there are many legal issues that may arise, especially for charitable organizations but also for not-for-profit organizations. A particularly difficult scenario may arise where one organization is a registered charity and the other is not. Whatever approach to a strategic alliance is taken — and there is merit in taking small steps to test the waters — lawyers and accountants should be involved. There is a need for a full canvas of the legal and accounting issues and for a solid documentation of the agreements that are reached, with supporting and background materials. The legal issues will be broad and can be far-reaching even with relatively small transactions. There may be a need for expertise in employment law, labour relations, tax law, trust law, corporate law and the law of real property. And both or all parties will need their own independent legal counsel. Without independent legal counsel, the directors would be hard-pressed to demonstrate that they exercised due diligence in the transaction on behalf of their organizations.

There will be a long list of areas that will need to be examined, in particular for those alliances that are closer to a merger than an advisory committee.[16] These areas run the gamut of the topics reviewed in this text, including:

---

16 See L.J.A. Greig & M. Elena Hoffstein, "Issues in Mergers and Fusions of Charitable Organizations" in *Fit to Be Tithed 2: Reducing Risks for Charities and Not-for-Profits* (Toronto: Law Society of Upper Canada, Continuing Legal Education, 1998), and J. Burke-Robertson, "Strategic Alli-

- review of the constating documents and incorporating statute or statutes to determine if there is the legal authority to do what is contemplated. A merger may be more difficult to achieve if one corporation is provincially incorporated and the other is federally incorporated under the *Canada Corporations Act*;
- review of financial position of the organizations and the financial ability of each to meet its obligations. This review would also include an analysis of any restricted funds or special purpose trusts, investment polices, insurance, outstanding litigation or contingencies for litigation;
- listing of assets, such as real property, personal property and intellectual property, with any encumbrances on the property;
- status of the organizations as corporations or otherwise to ensure, for example, that the corporation remains in existence and is in compliance with its incorporation legislation;
- review of compliance with any regulatory requirements, including those related to the environment, human rights, taxation (income, property, goods and services, retail), registration as a charity, employment-related statutes and any specific regulatory requirements for areas of activity of the charitable organizations;
- analysis of the legal rights of employees — whether in a unionized or non-unionized workplace. There may be complications where one workforce is unionized and the other is not or if there are different unions representing the employees. The analysis should include a review of various human resources policies, benefit plans (to ensure there are no outstanding liabilities that have not been accounted for or are not funded), outstanding grievances or similar proceedings, and status of payments for wages, salaries and vacation and remittances to governments for taxes and employment-related premiums and taxes;
- status of material contracts and with whom the contracts are. There may be opportunities for greater efficiency in administrative services, but those cost savings may be reduced substantially if there are long term leases that are "unbreakable" and result in significant operating expenses;
- regulatory approvals that are required — or regulatory agencies who would want to be informed early in the process. There may also be funding ministries, agencies or foundations that need to be consulted

---

ances in the Voluntary Sector in Canada", in *Fundamental New Developments in the Law of Charities in Canada* (Toronto: Canadian Bar Association–Ontario, 2000).

or advised in order to comply with the funding agreements. A major regulatory agency for charitable organizations will be Canada Customs and Revenue Agency and, in Ontario, the Public Guardian and Trustee.

The legal status of the organizations will have a bearing on many of these issues. For trusts to merge, for example, will require a court order and it may not be possible in law to obtain it. An application for *cy-pres* to change the objects of a trust is not necessarily approved by the court unless it can be shown that the charitable objects can no longer be fulfilled. For most trusts, it may be more fruitful to explore one of the less formal approaches to a strategic alliance. However, it may be possible for the trustees to obtain private legislation to accomplish the objectives. Similarly, with unincorporated associations, there may be difficulties in finding a sufficient legal authority to do what is desired unless the memoranda of association permit amendments and, preferably, amalgamations or strategic alliances.

E FOREIGN ACTIVITIES

Organizations may want to carry on activities outside of Canada. Provided that their constating documents are sufficiently broad to permit it, organizations can do so. The organization may, however, need to obtain legal status in that jurisdiction in order to operate legally in that jurisdiction. Many jurisdictions have some form of registration or licensing scheme to authorize an extra-territorial entity to operate in the jurisdiction.

There may be restrictions on the organization that make it difficult to operate outside Canada. For example, the letters patent may limit its operations to Canada; or it may be limited in using its assets outside of Canada. If the organization obtained a substantial portion of its assets using charitable gaming revenues, it may be prohibited from using those assets outside of the province as the funds are to be used for the benefit of the residents of the province.

Charitable organizations face other legal issues with respect to operations outside of Canada. There is no all-encompassing prohibition against charitable organizations carrying on their activities in other countries. But the organizations must meet certain requirements in order to do so legally for purposes of the *Income Tax Act* and maintain their registrations as charities under that Act. A charitable organization must use its assets to carry out its own charitable activities.

It is not always easy to determine how a charitable organization is carrying out its own activities in another country. In order to comply with the Act, the organization would normally do so:

- by using its own employees to carry out the work;
- by entering into a principal/agent agreement in which the agent agrees to be retained by the charitable organization and to act as its agent in carrying out the work and the specific duties assigned to it;
- by entering into contractual arrangements for others to carry out the work;
- by entering into other arrangements that will ensure that the charitable organization is accountable for how the resources are used with appropriate controls.

This last method is a relatively new approach and can be tied into joint venture agreements with government agencies, such as the Canadian International Development Agency. Any organization using this approach would also expect to be more closely monitored than organizations that use their own employees to carry out the work.[17] The Registered Charity Information Return requires additional information from the charitable organization each year about its activities and how those activities were carried out in foreign jurisdictions.

Fundamentally, the organization must be able to demonstrate that it is in control of its own resources and that it is directing how they are used. This fundamental principle is applicable to arrangements to operate outside Canada and to any strategic alliance within Canada. A charitable organization must be able to demonstrate to Canada Customs and Revenue Agency[18] that it meets the following requirements:

- the charity must maintain direction, control and supervision over the application of its funds by the agent;
- the charity's funds must remain apart from those of its agent so that the charity's role in any particular project or endeavour is separately identifiable as its own charitable activity;

---

[17] *A Better Tax Administration in Support of Charities: A Discussion Paper* (Ottawa: Minister of National Revenue, 1990). See also D. Amy, "Foreign Activities by Canadian Charities", in *Fundamental New Developments in the Law of Charities in Canada* (Toronto: Canadian Bar Association–Ontario, 2000).

[18] *Registered Charities: Operating a Registered Charity*, Information Circular IC 80-10R, December 17, 1985.

- the financial statements submitted in support of the charity's annual information returns must include a detailed breakdown of expenditures made in respect of the charitable activities performed on behalf of the charity by its agent(s);
- adequate books and records must be kept by the charity by its agent(s) to substantiate compliance with these conditions.

Generally, regardless of the legal approach taken by the various charitable organizations, the Canadian charity needs to show that:

- it has obtained reasonable assurances before entering into agreements with individuals or other organizations that they are able to deliver the services required by the charity. This assurance can be obtained by virtue of reputation, years of experience, expertise or by a due diligence investigation;
- all expenditures will further the Canadian charity's formal purpose and constitute charitable activities that the Canadian charity carries on itself;
- an adequate agreement is in place;
- the charity provides periodic, specific instructions to individuals or organizations as and when appropriate;
- the charity regularly monitors the progress of the project or program and can provide satisfactory evidence to Canada Customs and Revenue Agency;
- where appropriate, the charity makes periodic payments on the basis of the monitoring rather than lump sum payments and maintains the right to discontinue payments at any time if it is not satisfied.

An agreement must include the following elements:[19]

- the names and addresses of all parties;
- the duration of the agreement or the deadline by which the project must be completed;
- a description of the specific activities for which funds or other resources have been transferred, in sufficient detail to outline clearly the limits of the authority given to the recipient to act for the Canadian charity or on its behalf;

---

19 *Registered Charities: Operating Outside Canada*, RC4106, October 16, 2000.

- provision for written progress reports from the recipient of the charity's funds or other resources, or provision for the charity's right to inspect the project on reasonably short notice or both;
- provision that the Canadian charity will make payments by instalments based on confirmation of reasonable progress and that the resources provided to date have been applied to the specific activities outlined in the agreement;
- provision for withdrawing or withholding funds or other resources at the Canadian charity's discretion;
- provision for maintaining adequate records at the charity's address in Canada;
- in the case of agency agreements, provision for the Canadian charity's funds and property to be segregated from those of the agent and for the agent to keep separate books and records;
- the signatures of all parties and the date.

If the charitable organization participates in joint ventures with other organizations (Canadian or foreign) that advance its own charitable objects, a similar approach is necessary. It must be able to demonstrate that it exercises ongoing control in a joint venture through:

- presence of members of the Canadian charity on the governing body of the joint venture;
- presence in the field of members of the Canadian charity;
- joint control by the Canadian charity of foreign assets and property;
- input by the Canadian charity into the venture's initiation and follow-through, including the charity's ability to direct or modify the venture and to establish deadlines or other performance benchmarks;
- signature of the Canadian charity on loans, contracts, and other agreements arising from the venture;
- review and approval of the venture's budget by the Canadian charity, availability of an independent audit of the venture and the option to discontinue funding;
- authorship of procedures manuals, training guides, standards of conduct and so forth by the Canadian charity;
- on-site identification of the venture as being the work, at least in part, of the Canadian charity.

The requirements for a charitable organization to operate outside Canada are significant. There is a substantial investment at the start of any such initiative and on an ongoing basis in legal and accounting expertise. However, that investment does allow a Canadian charitable organization to have an influence beyond its size and own resources through appropriate organizational relationships with others.

F CARRYING ON REVENUE-GENERATING AND POLITICAL ACTIVITIES

Charitable and not-for-profit organizations are restricted in how they carry on revenue-generating activities. A fundamental position is that neither are intended to be "in business", that is to make and distribute profits. Charitable organizations are more severely restricted than are not-for-profit organizations in this regard.

Any revenue-generating activity must fall within the corporate objects of the organization, charitable or not-for-profit. In some cases it will be clearly in keeping with the purposes of the organization. For example, a not-for-profit organization that is intended to advance the interests of artists could operate a retail store. However, where the revenue-generating activity is more indirectly related to furthering the organizational mandate — for example, provision of a standard service or operation of a retail outlet offering regular merchandise with any surpluses generated returned to the organization — the rules are less clear. There may also be problems if the only artists who may use the retail store are members, especially if they receive "profits" from the operation. If any surpluses or profits are distributed to members, the organization would appear to have crossed over the line from being not-for-profit to becoming a for-profit or business entity.

Canada Customs and Revenue Agency takes the position that an organization will not be "non-profit" but "for-profit" if its principal activity is the carrying on of a business or trade.[20] It looks to the following factors in making its assessment of whether or not the activities of the not-for-profit organization are on the other side of the line:

- its activities are a trade or business in the ordinary meaning, that is, it is operated in a normal commercial manner;
- its goods or services are not restricted to members and their guests;
- it is operated on a profit basis rather than a cost recovery basis;
- it is operated in competition with taxable entities carrying on the same trade or business.

---

20 Interpretation Bulletin IT-496, Non-Profit Organizations, (February 18, 1983).

A charitable organization should also be able to illustrate how any revenue-generating activity is carrying out its charitable purposes. Historically, charitable organizations whose mandates are to relieve poverty have operated stores to sell low-cost clothing and other goods to the poor. But when does a charitable organization cross over the line if its primary market are not the poor but those with middle or high incomes who simply want cheaper goods?

Section 149.1(3)(a) of the *Income Tax Act* only permits a charity to carry on "related business activities".[21] What is or is not a related business is not always an easy thing to determine. No precise legal test has been established to determine what is and what is not a related business activity. The former Revenue Canada (now Canada Customs and Revenue Agency) attempted to provide clarification in its 1990 Discussion Paper[22] on charities. It commented that if the business activity does not become a "substantial commercial endeavour" the activity will be considered related if:

- the activity is related to the charity's objects or ancillary to them;
- there is no private profit motive since any net revenues will be used for charitable purposes;
- the business operation does not compete directly with other for-profit businesses;[23]
- the business has been in operation for some time and is accepted by the community.

Under section 149.1 (1) of the *Income Tax Act*, a related business is defined to include "a business that is unrelated to the objects of the charity if substantially all persons employed by the charity in the carrying on of that business are not remunerated for that employment". CCRA interprets "substantially all" to mean 90% or more. Accordingly, an organization may also carry on non-integral business activity without jeopardising its charitable registration provided the activity is 90% volunteer run. So, for example, an organization can operate a volunteer

---

21 *Alberta Institute on Mental Retardation v. Canada*, [1987] 3 F.C. 286 (F.C.A.) may have extended the circumstances for business activities to include for fundraising purposes. However, this case may not be as expansive as initially considered.

22 *A Better Tax Administration in Support of Charities.*

23 CCRA and this approach do not address a developing issue – what happens to this criteria where the business activity of the charitable organization creates a new industry or commercial activity and for-profit businesses subsequently occupy the field? Arguably, this situation has occurred with respect to used clothing and household goods.

carwash as a fundraiser even if such activity is not contemplated in its mandate.

In Ontario, the *Charitable Gifts Act*[24] and the *Charities Accounting Act*[25] place significant obstacles to a charitable organization operating businesses that do not have a clear relationship to the charitable objects of the organization. Section 2 of the *Charitable Gifts Act* prohibits most charities in Ontario from owning more than ten per cent interest in a business. If the charity does so, it must divest itself of the excess within seven years.

The *Charities Accounting Act* requires a charity to sell any real property that it does not use for charitable purposes and use the proceeds for its charitable purposes. As a result, with few exceptions such as hospitals that are governed by other statutory schemes in Ontario, most charitable organizations would not be able to hold real property for investment purposes, such as an apartment building or commercial building. It may be able to lease out some surplus space in its own building which is otherwise used for its charitable activities, but care must be taken even in that case.

Political activities pose another problem for charitable organizations. Lobbying and advocating for political change is not a charitable activity. There are some recognized exceptions to this general statement; for example, a child welfare agency may lobby for changes to child welfare legislation to a reasonable extent.[26] Not-for-profit organizations are not limited in this area and there are a number of organizations that lobby and carry out significant political activities as part of their mandates. Where a not-for-profit organization's mandate includes lobbying, directors should be cognizant of the need to comply with federal and provincial legislative requirements governing registration of lobbying activity or/or lobbyists.

There are obvious restrictions, but are there any options to permit from a broader context, the organization to carry out either business or political activities? To a limited extent, there are some models that may do so and allow for a level of activities that could not occur within the charitable or not-for-profit organization. However, the board of directors ought to receive legal and accounting advice and ensure that

---

24 R.S.O. 1990, c. C.8.

25 R.S.O. 1990, c. C.10.

26 See several Canada Customs and Revenue Agency publications for further discussion of this issue, including, *Registered Charities: Political Objects and Activities*, Information Circular 78-3; *Registered Charities – Ancillary and Incidental Political Activities*, Information Circular 87-1; and *Registered Charities: Education, Advocacy and Political Activities*, RC4107 (Draft).

operationally there are clear distinctions made and maintained between the charitable or not-for-profit organization and the business or political entity. The issues discussed above about control and piercing the corporate veil are relevant factors to consider in structuring any such relationships.

The major options available for business activities[27] include the following:

- business corporation. A business corporation could be used to carry out any business activity. This option is available to both charitable and not-for-profit organizations, but the method implementing this option will vary as between the two, especially for charitable organizations in Ontario. A thorough review of the income tax implications would need to be made to ensure that any tax liability in the hands of the business corporation is minimized, either through an appropriate level of donations to the registered charity or through the size of the corporation.
  In the case of the charitable organization, it may be able to structure the ownership of the shares through intermediaries to avoid the restrictions in the *Charitable Gifts Act*. For example, a not-for-profit corporation could be incorporated to hold the shares of the business corporation and, in turn, forward the "profits" to the charitable organization. However, this type of scheme may be seen as a sham and that statute does purport to extend to direct and indirect ownership. But it may still be possible to work from within the statutory scheme, e.g., hold the shares for up to seven years or have several charitable and not-for-profit organizations each hold less than ten per cent of the shares.
- business trust — a business trust is also a taxable entity under the *Income Tax Act* but it can be used to make distributions to charitable or not-for-profit organizations, which are not taxable entities. One difficulty with this option is that the trustees would be exposed to personal liability, which could be a significant deterrent. There are also timing limits to the use of a business trust. Every 21 years, there will be a deemed realization of the assets, which may trigger capital gains.

27 See J. Burke-Robertson, "Charities Carrying on Business Activities – The Legal Considerations" in *Fit to be Tithed 2: Reducing Risks for Charities and Not-for-Profits* (Toronto: Law Society of Upper Canada, 1998).

Both of these options may also give rise to other complications with respect to goods and services taxation, potential liability for the charitable or not-for-profit organization or its directors (especially if not all the procedures are followed and maintained), and ongoing maintenance and record-keeping. Depending upon the type of business that is established, there may also be employment law, environmental law, tax law, regulatory law, securities law and other statutory and common law concerns that need to be addressed. The board also needs to be concerned with the *Income Tax Act*'s provisions with respect to anti-avoidance measures.

Neither of these options should be considered without expert legal and accounting advice and only if the potential benefits exceed the costs and potential costs. In addition, the payment of that legal and accounting advice needs to be justified as a reasonable and necessary expense for purposes of the charitable organization.

Appendix I

BOARD DEVELOPMENT COMMITTEE

Terms of Reference

Purpose:

The Board Development Committee is a Standing Committee of the Board whose membership is approved by the Board. It ensures the stability and health of the organization through recruitment and development of strong, stable, and effective leadership. Its key responsibility is to present to the membership at the Annual Meeting, a slate of nominees for election to the Board. It is also responsible for the orientation and development of Board members, and for ongoing Board Governance issues, including the evaluation of Board effectiveness.

Functions:

- Determine specific skill, ability and representation needs of the Board.
- Actively recruit and maintain a roster of potential Board and Committee Members, utilizing a regular consultation process with major constituencies (clients, funders, board, staff and other stakeholders).
- Recommend candidates to the Board at the Annual General Meeting, and also candidates to fill vacancies that occur during the year on the Board or Executive.
- Prepare in consultation with incumbent Officers and Committee Chairs, a slate of Officers and Committee Chairs to be elected at the first Board meeting following the Annual Meeting, and to recommend to the Board, individuals to be elected as Committee Chairs during the year as required.
- Evaluate the eligibility for re-election of persons on the Board whose terms are expiring.
- Implement systems for evaluation of Board members.
- Implement systems for evaluation of Board effectiveness.
- Ensure adequacy of Board orientation systems.

- Consider and evaluate Board governance, and make recommendations to the Board as appropriate.

Composition and Quorum:

The Board Development Committee shall consist of three to five members of the Board in addition to the Chair (who shall be a member of the Board, normally the Past Chair), one or two community members, plus the current Chair of the Board and President serving as ex-officio members. A quorum shall be four members.

Members of the Board on the Committee shall include members with three or more years' experience on the Board, as well as members with only one or two years' experience on the Board. The Committee should reflect major organizational constituencies.

Accountability:

The Board Development Committee reports to the general membership at the Annual General Meeting with regard to its nominations to the Board. For all other responsibilities, the Committee is accountable to the Board.

Term of Office:

Members of the Board Development Committee shall hold office for one year or until a new Committee has been established.

FINANCE & AUDIT COMMITTEE

Terms of Reference

Purpose:

The Finance & Audit Committee will review audit, budget and financial activities on behalf of the Board, and will provide liaison between the Board and the external auditors.

Functions:

- Review the annual Audited Financial Statements before submission to the Board. The auditor has the right to appear before and to be heard by any meeting of this Committee called to discuss internal controls of the organization or the audited financial statements.

- Review audit fee arrangements and advise the Board on the appointment of auditors.
- Review the operating and capital budgets of the organization for the following year, and make recommendations therein to the Board.
- Provide recommendations on internal control practices and administrative procedures. Review insurance coverage of the organization and make appropriate recommendations.

Composition:

The Committee will be comprised of not fewer than three members of the Board. The Vice Chairman/Treasurer, the President and the Chairs of the working committees will be ex-officio members of the Committee.

Accountability:

The Finance and Audit Committee is accountable to the Board.

Term of Office:

Members of the Finance and Audit Committee shall hold office for one year or until a new Committee has been established.

CONFLICT OF INTEREST POLICY

Board/Committee Members

At no time may any member of the Board or a committee consider a matter where a possible conflict of interest arises.

Conflict of interest occurs when Board or committee members participate in discussion or decision-making about a matter from which they, or someone with whom they have a close personal relationship, may directly or indirectly benefit, regardless of the size of the benefit. A conflict of interest also arises where a Board or committee member has a past, current or contemplated future involvement in a volunteer, staff or professional capacity with an external organization and participates in discussion or decision-making about a matter that potentially affects that organization.

Where there is a question as to the existence of a possible conflict of interest, the Board or committee member should consult the Chair of the Board or committee, as appropriate. The chair may opt to put the matter to the entire Board or committee for consideration, if he or she chooses or at the request of the Board or committee member.

Any possible conflict of interest on the part of a Board or committee member shall be disclosed to the Board or Committee. When any such interest becomes a matter of Board or committee action, the person shall not vote or use personal influence on the matter and shall not be counted in the quorum for decisions at a meeting at which action is being taken on the interest. The Minutes of all actions taken on such matters shall clearly reflect that these requirements have been met.

EXECUTIVE DIRECTOR PERFORMANCE APPRAISAL

Note: This evaluation protocol assumes a close correlation between CEO performance and organization performance.

Terms of Reference

Purpose:

1. Evaluation of Executive Director and Organization performance
2. Clarity of expectations and communication between Executive Director and the Board
3. Executive Director development and improvement
4. Compliance with accreditation standards for Board performance

Method:

Measure Organization performance, i.e., achievement of goals and operation of organization within Board parameters relating to the following categories:

- Service Delivery
- Financial Management
- Asset Management
- Human Resources Management
- Community Representation/Accountability
- Community Leadership

Planning Phase:

- Planning documents are prepared annually by the Organization for Board consideration and approval Performance indicators for each category (see above) are set annually by the Board. These documents should set out the organization's mandate in terms of both ends and means for the upcoming fiscal/operational year.

Monitoring Phase:

- Monitoring Reports (performance in relation to indicators) are submitted to the Board quarterly by the Executive Director for annual goals and annually for three to five year goals.

Evaluation Phase:

- Performance documents are prepared annually by the Organization for the Board.
- A formal appraisal of the Executive Director is conducted approximately two to three months after the end of each fiscal/operational year with a written report to the Human Resource file by the Board President and Senior Vice-President or immediate Past President, as applicable.

Additional Possible Components:

- Integrate Organization Planning Cycle with external funding submission(s).
- Incorporate staff evaluation of management.
- Incorporate community input re: organization performance.

Planning Documents
(assumes March 31st year end)

Environmental Scan	Fall
Strategic Priorities, three to five years	Fall
Service and Financial Plan	Winter
Capital Budget	Winter

Evaluation/Monitoring Reports

Monitoring Reports

• Compliance Reports	as per Monitoring Schedule
• Quarterly Financial Statements	as per Monitoring Schedule
• Quarterly Service Reports	as per Monitoring Schedule

Evaluation Report

- Year End Financial Report — May/ June
- Year End Service Report — May/ June

Annual Performance Interview

Executive Director

1. A brief summary of achievements/compliance with Executive parameters for the past year will be prepared separately by the E.D. and the Board representatives prior to the meeting.
2. Summaries will be exchanged at the meeting and, if indicated, related plans will be defined.

   Examples:

   i) The Board to make more explicit an expectation or executive parameter;
   ii) The CEO to provide an action plan to meet an expectation or stay within an executive parameter.

3. What major challenges arose during the year and how did you deal with them?
4. Comment on your performance relative to E.D./Board relationships — consider all relevant policies.
5. Comment upon your personal professional development initiatives and needs.
6. What recommendations do you have for the Board to assist/support you over the coming year?

PROGRAM AND INITIATIVES PRESENTATIONS GUIDELINES

Terms of Reference

Purpose:

To increase Board awareness of:

- Which Ends (results/outcomes) the program/initiative seeks to accomplish. Specifically, how does the program/initiative address the key questions, "What Good, Which People, What Cost?"

- Issues that potentially require Board involvement or setting of parameters.

Preparation:

- A written program/initiative summary (format below, one to two pages maximum) to be sent out with Board mailings that occur prior to the Board meeting date.
- Verbal presentation at Board meeting. Total time on agenda of 20 minutes. Used to focus on issues, not a repeat of the written material which members will have been expected to read prior to attending meeting.

Format:

The following framework is meant to be a focus for the program/initiative presentation, not a restriction. As time is limited, the framework helps keep the focus on the key areas of your program/initiative that need to be discussed with Board members. Feel free to choose who/how to make the presentation as best fits the program/initiative.

FOR WHOM

- what is the scope of the program or initiative (what clients, communities, partners are involved?)
- what changes are occurring?
- any gaps?

FOR WHAT GOOD

- what are the Ends (results/outcomes) that the Board has agreed are to be achieved by this program/initative?
- what is known about the impact/outcomes of the program/initiative?
- what evaluation methods were/are used?

MISSION/SERVICE CONTINUUM

- where does the program/initiative fit within the organization's mandate?
- are the means of implementing the program in keeping with the organization's practices/values?

COST

– financial, staff and volunteer resources used to deliver the program/initiative.

ISSUES

– spotlight those issues that Board needs to be aware of that are relevant to its major constituencies (clients, funders, staff and other stakeholders).

MONITORING SCHEDULE – BOARD

(assumes March 31st year end)

	Completion Dates
Documents signed by President/CEO/Executive Director	Sept/Dec/Mar/Jun
Organization Service, Financial and Capital Plan	March
Quarterly Reports to Board	Sept/Nov/Feb/Jun
Year End Service, Financial and Capital Reports	June
Performance Appraisal, Executive Director	June
Executive Director Compensation Review	June
Board Strategic Priorities	Dec
Board Workplan	Dec
By-laws Review	April
Committee Reports: Finance & Audit Committee	April
Board Development Committee	Dec
Fundraising Committee	Oct
Volunteer Committee	June
Policy Reviews: I. Mission, Ends	Annually
II. 2. Board Job Description	Every 2 yrs.*
II. 1. Governing Style	Every 2 yrs.*
II. 4. Committee Principles	Every 2 yrs.*
II. 5. Directors' Code of Conduct	Every 2 yrs.*
II. 3. Chairperson's Role	Every 2 yrs.*
III. 2. CEO Job Description	Every 3 yrs. or with new hire
III. 3. Monitoring CEO Performance	Every 3 yrs.
IV. 2. Staff & Volunteer Treatment	Every 3 yrs.
IV. 5. Executive Succession	Every 3 yrs.
IV. 6. Asset Protection	Every 3 yrs.
IV. 7. Compensation & Benefits	Every 3 yrs.
IV. 8. Communication & Counsel to Board	Every 3 yrs.
IV. 4. Financial Condition	Every 3 yrs.

IV. 3. Financial Planning	Every 3 yrs.
III. 1. Delegation to CEO	Every 3 yrs.
IV. 1. General Executive Parameters	Every 3 yrs.
IV. 9. Advocacy & Public Relations	Every 3 yrs.
IV. 10. Joint Ventures	Every 3 yrs.
IV. 12. Services	Every 3 yrs.

* Review in first meeting chaired by new President

GOOD PRACTICE GUIDE FOR EFFECTIVE STEWARDSHIP ANALYSIS* — September 1999		
Mission and Strategic Planning	**What do we have in place?**	**Action Needed**
• establish the mission; communicate it with members and stakeholders; and periodically review its appropriateness		
• approve a process for risk assessment and management to assist the board in anticipating risk, assessing it, and managing the outcome of risky actions		
• oversee and monitor the achievement of the mission by setting measurable goals, defined in terms of desired outcomes or impacts on clients, rather than as inputs or activities		
Transparency and Communication	**What do we have in place?**	**Action Needed**
• establish policies for communicating and receiving feedback from stakeholders		

* This document was prepared by Lois Hollstedt, Executive Director of the Vancouver Young Women's Christian Association.

Transparency and Communication	What do we have in place?	Action Needed
• ensure, as part of a code of ethical conduct, that the complaints and grievance procedure works effectively		
• hold regular board meetings that provide an opportunity for discussion		
• provide a collective memory of the organization by ensuring that appropriate minutes and documents are kept		
• respond appropriately to requests for information		
Structures	**What do we have in place?**	**Action Needed**
• a board capable of providing objective oversight		
• an independent nominating committee to ensure the appropriate succession of the board		
• an audit committee, whose primary responsibility is to report whether the organization is in compliance with the laws, rules, regulations and contracts that govern it. It reviews whether the management, information and control systems are organized and implemented to carry out these rules and regulations, and as well is responsible for supervising external financial reporting		

The Board's Understanding of its Role	What do we have in place?	Action Needed
• decide upon and communicate its philosophy of governance, *i.e.*, "policy governance" by making policy and providing strategic direction, but keeping hands off management or "administrative" board (which not only sets policy, but does some implementation itself). The former is preferred in larger organizations, but requires professional management		
• develop a code of conduct for board members to help directors understand, and ensure they agree to the obligations which they are undertaking		
• establish and enforce written conflict of interest policy governing board members and staff or volunteers who have independent decision-making authority over the resources of the organization		
• provide job descriptions for board members that outline general duties and how the board's work will be evaluated		
• invest in board orientation and ongoing information sessions		
• recognize contribution of board members and provide feedback on the board's performance		
• use the time of the board members efficiently		

Fiscal Responsibility	What do we have in place?	Action Needed
• approve a budget that reflects the organization's priorities and is based on realistic assumptions (of revenues, costs, and other factors such as inflation)		
• monitor and control expenditures, based on appropriate accounting procedures		
• oversee stewardship of organization's assets and liabilities		
• registered charity oversight of issuance and record-keeping of receipts for charitable donations		
• approve annual reports, including financial statements		
Oversight of Human Resources	**What do we have in place?**	**Action Needed**
• ensure organization complies with employment legislation, work place safety regulations and reviews its employment arrangements periodically to ensure they comply with good practice		
• ensure staff are provided with job descriptions, orientation, management, training and performance appraisals		
• recruit staff openly, fairly and systematically		
• review periodically the staff structure and effectiveness of working relationship between the board and staff		

Volunteers	What do we have in place?	Action Needed
• have a clear set of policies regarding recruitment, preparation, oversight and recognition of volunteers; (programs should be designed and assessed with same stringency as other programs)		
• give volunteers a clear statement of the tasks and activities that they are to carry out, perhaps including job descriptions or volunteer agreements		
• adopt and adhere to codes of ethical conduct for managers of volunteers and volunteers		
• provide adequate orientation, training and evaluation		
• publicly recognize the contributions of volunteers		
• screen volunteers, particularly if the organization works with vulnerable populations		
• provide direction and, in unionized environments, work with the unions to reach agreement, on how the paid or non-voluntary volunteers are to be integrated into the organization		
• establish explicit expectations about the claiming of expenses		

Assessment and Control Systems	What do we have in place?	Action Needed
• a code of ethical conduct and an effective monitoring and complaints procedure; (a sample code of ethical conduct appears in Appendix II)		
• a framework for internal regulations, including constitution and bylaws (might be quite simple in small organizations)		
• a compliance audit as an integral part of the annual evaluation cycle to check that the rules governing the organization are being followed and that control systems are functioning and adequate; (normally supervised by the audit committee. The board's responsibility is to respond, indicating how it has addressed issues of noncompliance identified by the committee)		
• evaluation of the performance of the board collectively		
Planning for Succession and Diversity	**What do we have in place?**	**Action Needed**
• discuss if representation of users and constituencies on board is important to mission and credibility and, if appropriate, work toward increasing diversity, ensuring representation is not token		

Public Reporting on Good Governance	What do we have in place?	Action Needed
• provide certain information to the federal government about its governance, programs and finances		
• adhere to code of ethical fundraising – Canadian Centre for Philanthropy, or similar that is publicly available		
• practice transparency — respond appropriately to complaints and requests for information by the public, members or clients		
Required Reporting: The Basics	**What do we have in place?**	**Action Needed**
• description of the organization's mission, programs and intended results		
• financial statements, as approved by the board		
• description of fundraising activities over past year including amount of revenues and amount spent raising them		
• description of basic governance structures, including board size and methods for selecting board members		
• disclosure of the code of ethical fundraising to which the organization adheres		
• description of the organization's approach to responding to complaints		
• how to get further information directly from the organization		

Requirements for Larger Organizations	What do we have in place?	Action Needed
• the nature of the mission, intended outcomes and strategic planning processes		
• overview of policies for transparency, code of ethical conduct, complaints process, number of board meetings per year		
• description of governing structures, including whether an independent nominating and an audit committee exist		
• summary of the methods of board stewardship		
• evidence of fiscal responsibility, as through provision of audited financial statements		
• methods for board succession and diversity of representation (if applicable)		

Index

T

V